WILDERNESS

A Stepping Stone to the Greatness of God

Rick Sizemore

TALL WOOD

PUBLISHING HOUSE

Wilderness: A Stepping Stone to the Greatness of God
© Copyright 2015 - 2019 Rick Sizemore

Revised Second Edition

Tall Wood Publishing House
PO Box 8
Pembroke, Virginia 24136

Cover photo copyright © by Jeff Greenough

ISBN 13: 978-1-57688-072-2 (print)
ISBN 13: 978-1-57688-073-9 (ebook)

Printed in the United States of America

This book is dedicated to the Lord
for His faithfulness to me in the wilderness
seasons of my life.

It is also dedicated to
my brother, Buddy Sizemore,
who now lives in Heaven and was a continual
inspiration to me.

Acknowledgments

I am a man most blessed. My treasure chest is full to overflowing when I think of all those who have poured into me as I journey through this life. Yes, this has been a journey with numerous wilderness experiences, but it has been those precious gems that made the endurance worth every step.

My beloved wife, Paula, has been so faithful as we've walked through the various seasons of life. Her love and devotion, as well as her strength in Jesus, has kept me going even in the roughest of those seasons.

Shea, Michele and Lile so bless my heart and have helped me understand the heart of our heavenly Father. They are priceless jewels.

I am constantly reminded of the Father's love through my grandchildren, Maks and Frances. I see the heart of the heavenly Father through my Dad, who has been so faithful and loves me so unconditionally.

My treasure chest is filled with other jewels, among them the faithful elders, brothers and sisters of Dwelling Place Christian Fellowship who have faithfully loved me and my family for these many years.

I am truly a blessed writer because of all these gems the Lord has brought to me out of my wilderness journeys.

Rick Sizemore

Table of Contents

Foreword

Have you ever felt like you were wandering in the desert aimlessly? Have you ever felt like all your props have been pulled out from underneath you? Well, you are not alone. Every person has experienced some type of wilderness at some point in life, whether he or she could identify it as such or not. That is what makes this book a must-read!

The Lord has gifted Rick to teach His Word, and I have benefited extensively from his gifting over the many years I have known him. Many previously wounded areas in my heart have been healed as a result of Rick's teachings on a practical approach to releasing God's truth. This book is no different. Rick breaks down the various types of wildernesses we might experience, as well as how and when we experience these wildernesses in our lives. In the process, he brings truth about who Father God is and helps us understand the purpose of the wilderness experience. That revelation and understanding enable us to enter our promised land and the destinies Father God has for us.

Rick, thank you for writing this book. I have experienced a few different types of wildernesses, and as I write this foreword, I am currently going through a wilderness of transition. I am grateful for the wealth of knowledge God has placed in you and your passion for the personal revelation of truth about Father God that brings healing, growth, and freedom to our lives.

— Carla Howard
Elder, Two Rivers Church, Gilbert, Arizona

Introduction

I have always loved surprises. Surprises can be exciting—think of Christmas, birthdays, and the kindness of special friends.

But when it comes to the adversities of life, a surprise can be devastating to our faith and the stability of our hearts. When we collide headfirst with adversity, the world seems to turn upside down, and if we are unprepared for it, the adversity can shipwreck our faith.

Early in my Christian walk, I would cycle through disillusionment whenever life grew difficult. As the Lord started maturing me, I realized I had a "movie mindset." All the good, old-time movies I liked had happy endings. The conclusion of each film projected a perfect conclusion for the main characters, and I caught myself looking for the happily-ever-after in my own life. *The Empire Strikes Back* really disturbed me when I first saw it because it didn't have the ending I wanted. There was no happy ending, just a continuation of struggle. Who wanted an "ending" that wasn't happy?

Slowly, God began to alter my sense of reality. He helped me understand that adversities are part of living in a fallen world. It isn't that there is no happy ending in life—it is that He causes us to live in victory.

> *". . . so that no one would be disturbed by these afflictions; for you yourselves know that we have been destined for this. For indeed when we were with you, we kept telling you in advance that we were going to suffer affliction; and so it came to pass, as you know."*   — 1 Thessalonians 3:3–4

In this passage, the apostle Paul didn't want hardship to catch the Thessalonian Christians by surprise. He was concerned enough about their walk with God that he sent Timothy to find out how their faith had fared in difficulty.

The important question is not, "Will we go through adversities?" Yes, we will. Jesus warned of what we could expect in this world: *"These things I have spoken to you, so that in Me you may have peace. In the world you have tribulation, but take courage; I have overcome the world"* (John 16:33). But here is the key: Even though we face adversities, through Jesus we can walk victoriously. All of us need to take that truth and bury it deep in our hearts as a firm foundation.

This book was written in hopes that none of us would be caught by surprise. God's heart is that we would be like the wise man who built his house upon the rock. When the storms of life come, we don't have to be caught off guard. We can face the pressure and uncertainty of adversity, seeking shelter in the Lord's comfort and His promise to provide for us.

Getting Your Needs Met in Jesus

In order to overcome the adversities we will certainly face, we need to be prepared. We are able to stand our ground in the storm when our needs are filled and firmly rooted in Jesus Christ. If our needs are met in Jesus, we can walk through any uncertainty the physical world could hand us. We can face adversity with confidence, knowing we can overcome it.

> *"For whatever is born of God overcomes the world; and this is the victory that has overcome the world — our faith."*
> — 1 John 5:4

This brings us to the topic of the book. A wilderness is one of the major ways in which the Lord teaches us to bring our needs to Him so we can be saturated with His fullness. All of us have experienced or will experience some type of wilderness in our lives. The great men and women of God written about in

His Word all experienced these times of uncertainty and solitude—but it was in these times that the fullness of God was
established in their hearts. When the adversities of life hit, these
heroes of the faith were able to depend fully on God, who was
a reliable Source to save and sustain them. That dependency on
God, worth more than gold, was birthed in times of wilderness.

The wilderness is a concept found in both testaments. Before and during Jesus' ministry, He experienced at least two
different types of wildernesses.[1] Abraham, the father of our
faith, experienced a wilderness when he left his family home
and went to the land the Lord had promised to him. Joseph experienced a long series of wildernesses as he matured from an
annoying little brother to a ruler of Egypt. After his conversion,
Paul went into the wilderness of the Arabian desert, where he
was prepared as an apostle to the Gentiles.

I could go on and on, but my point is that every man and
woman of God passes through some type of wilderness, and
during these times, we have the opportunity to meet God in
ways that change the heart and blow the mind.

Establishing Your Faith

A wilderness, like an adversity, can shake our faith if we don't
understand it. The children of Israel didn't understand the wilderness they encountered as they journeyed from the Red Sea
to Mount Sinai. They had just seen God rescue them in miraculous ways—why had He now led them out into the desert? As
a result of their lack of knowledge, defeat and unbelief began to
mark their relationship with the Lord.

Similarly, King Saul didn't understand the wilderness he
faced during his time at Gilgal, and in the end, his faith was
shaken and he sinned.[2]

Jesus, on the other hand, understood the wilderness He
faced at the beginning of His ministry; therefore, His life and
ministry were established. In the same way, we can face wildernesses with knowledge and understanding and consequently
experience the greatness that follows.

Recognizing when we are in a wilderness helps us stay calm and keep our eyes on the Lord. A few years ago, the Lord showed me that three precious women in our church were about to encounter a season of wilderness. He told me it would be a time when He spoke to them about His lovingkindness[3] and that when they came out of the wilderness, they would be "leaning" on the Lord.[4] No one wants to be told that difficult times are coming, and when I first shared this word with them, these women were upset with me. But as time progressed, all three experienced a season that aligned with the word I had spoken. Knowing what was happening helped them navigate their hearts, and the fruit of God's lovingkindness manifested in their lives. All three women have vibrant relationships with the Lord.

All of us face seasons of wilderness. Some of those seasons are relatively short — they can look like a rough afternoon when your car is in the shop, your rental gets a flat, and you're late for an important meeting. Some seasons of wilderness are longer and can last for days or potentially even years. In every wilderness, we have the opportunity to come to Jesus to have our needs met completely.

In this book, we will address these questions and several others:

* Where is God in the wilderness, and what is
   He doing with us?
* What are the purposes of a wilderness?
* How should we respond in a wilderness?

My heart in writing this book is that each of us would understand the reality and purpose of the different seasons the Bible calls the wilderness. When we understand the type of wilderness we are experiencing, we can know how to respond. We can direct our thoughts and faith through the season and come out on the other side enriched and empowered to live life to the fullest.

Here, however, before you turn to the first chapter, I need to make a disclaimer. Sometimes when people try to teach about the wilderness, or what some have termed "the dark night of the soul," the topic comes across in a way that makes it seem clear and concise, when it isn't. Life is complex and fluid. Every type of wilderness we experience can be intertwined with other elements and situations, potentially making the road forward a little difficult to perceive. Though the wilderness is not necessarily a time that is easy to comprehend, I will do my best to make the topic as clear as possible.

Notes / Reference Scriptures

1. Matthew 4:1; Luke 5:15-16
2. 1 Samuel 13
3. Hosea 2:14
4. Song of Solomon 8:5

PART ONE

An Introduction to the Wilderness

A Time of Revelation and Preparation

"Every good thing given and every perfect gift is from above, coming down from the Father of lights, with whom there is no variation or shifting shadow." — James 1:17

God does not vary from giving us good things. Just as He is always good, so He always gives good gifts.

In the first section of this book, we are going to look at what a wilderness is, what it isn't, and how God is our loving Father in every circumstance we face. His Word is relevant, sustaining, satisfying, and fresh in every wilderness. If He has led us into a wilderness, we can rest assured that it will be a good thing.

1 The Wilderness Season

In 1986 my wife, Paula, and I responded to God's call to go into full-time ministry. We left our newly built custom home, our home church, a vibrant ministry to the youth in our area, and the security of our business to move to a city we had never visited before. Everything was different—the weather, the lifestyle, the relationships, the church, and the time demands of seminary and family. We went from living in a nice new house to renting an outdated, very small two-bedroom apartment. We jumped from financial security to financial uncertainty. We went from leading ministries to youth to doing hardly any ministry. In many ways, it was a very dry season in our lives. We were stretched in just about every area, and it was hard. But when we look back on that time of wilderness, we realize it was one of the most important seasons in our lives. It propelled us into the ministry we are still in today.

Simply defined, a wilderness, also called the dark night of the soul, is any time a source of comfort or psychological balance is removed, and we can no longer rely on anything other than Jesus to meet our needs. It can be a difficult time, but hindsight is twenty-twenty. When we look back, we often can see the hand of God and understand why He allowed certain things to happen in our lives.

Wilderness is a term found throughout the Bible, from Genesis to Revelation. There are different types of wildernesses, but each type can be summarized in the following way:

A wilderness is a place, circumstance, or time
of no known human props or sources to stabilize our souls.

The key phrase here is "no known human props and sources." In a wilderness, we are given the opportunity to realize that Jesus is the only Source we need. He is our Provider, our Protector, and the Giver and Sustainer of our lives. He is the One who meets all our needs.

When God led the Hebrews through the desert (a physical wilderness), He miraculously provided for them. He gave them food that was unique. It wasn't something they or their fathers had known,[1] and they couldn't explain it. Almost every single thing they experienced in the desert was new to them. Their provision came from God's hand alone, and they couldn't rely on any of the worldly resources they had used in the past. Without God, they had nothing.

Have you ever been in a similar position? Have you experienced a season in which nothing happened according to your expectations? You couldn't control anything. You couldn't predict anything. If your hope is not firmly fixed to Jesus, the wilderness can be a tough time.

Yet in every wilderness we go through, God is doing a great work in our hearts. The fruit of His work during a wilderness is incredible. It brings stability to our faith. The wilderness allows the fullness of His blessing to be eternally established in our lives. When we encounter a wilderness, we can joyously expect good things—both while we are in the wilderness and when we reach the other side.

As we get into this study of wildernesses, we need to remember a few important things: God is good, and He gives good gifts. He disciplines those He loves. He will not abandon us in hard times—He will provide for us. In the wilderness, He reminds us of the promises He has made us, and He speaks to us again. Let's look at each of these points more closely.

God Is Good

"Surely God is good to Israel,
To those who are pure in heart!" — Psalm 73:1

"But as for me, the nearness of God is my good;
I have made the Lord God my refuge,
That I may tell of all Your works." — Psalm 73:28

In a wilderness, the first truth we have to establish in our hearts is the truth that God is good. He is sincerely, completely, absolutely good. When we understand that God is good, we can take refuge in Him in the midst of hardship.[2] We won't take refuge in God if we don't understand that He is good.

He is a good Father, who gives good gifts:

"Every good thing given and every perfect gift is from above, coming down from the Father of lights, with whom there is no variation or shifting shadow." — James 1:17

God does not vary from giving us good things. Just as He is always good, so He always gives good gifts. When we miss that important truth, the wilderness can make us bitter. Even though a wilderness can be a painful time, we should think about the experience in this way:

If the Lord is good,
and He gives only good gifts,
and He is somehow involved with the wilderness,
then the wilderness has to be something good.

Obviously, this foundation doesn't make the wilderness an "easy" experience, yet within the context of God's fullness, a divinely ordained wilderness can save our lives and open the door to the promised land.

God Disciplines Those He Loves

Every good father trains his children to live life successfully. The second truth is that: in the wilderness, God "disciplines" those He loves. In its purest form, discipline is a very positive thing. When most people think of discipline, they think of punishment, but the Greek word for "discipline" is paideuei, which literally means to train or teach. It does not mean punishment. Discipline can involve a form of punishment only when it is used to teach a child the difference between right and wrong. The child, obviously, doesn't find the training and teaching — discipline — very joyous, but for the father and mother, it is an expression of love and acceptance because they are empowering their child to grow up.[3]

Deuteronomy 8 is dedicated to instruction concerning the wilderness — the "dry" season, when the ground appears dead and barren, and we don't know what we are doing or how to make things work. Verse 5 gives an important clue about the Father's heart for every dry season we encounter: "Thus you are to know in your heart that the Lord your God was disciplining you just as a man disciplines his son." A wilderness is not a time of punishment but a time to be taught life-changing and foundational truths.

When I graduated from college, I went to work for my dad. He was the president and part owner of a chain of grocery stores. I graduated with a business degree, with an emphasis in banking and finance, and I was looking forward to administrating the company's finances. I could see myself earning a large salary, sitting at a nice desk, making large financial evaluations, and deciding the direction of the company based on those evaluations.

On my first day of work, I met with my dad to discuss my salary and role in the company. It didn't take long for my inflated visions of greatness to be brought back to earth. My dad informed me that my first assignment was to take the machete out of the back of his car and clear an acre lot adjacent to one of our stores. Many of the weeds were eight feet tall. I cut and hacked for about two weeks in the hot Florida sun, and the whole time, I wondered why in the world I had gone to college so I could cut down weeds.

Once I finished that task, I "graduated" to scraping paint off the ice merchandising machines. Then I moved on to sweeping and washing down spiderwebs from storefronts. This task often left me soaking wet and covered in webs that had collapsed from the overhangs. These odd jobs went on for months. Finally, the day came when I was told to dress nicely for my next day of work — but when I arrived the following morning, I was not assigned to the accountant's office. Instead, I had been given the lowest position in the company: that of cashier. Not only that, but they put me in the slowest store in the whole chain.

As the years progressed, I went through about every job in the company, from the dirtiest job to one of the more complicated jobs: that of investing large sums of money on a weekly basis; eventually I became a part owner in the company. After about eight years of working alongside my father, we sold Time Saver Food Stores as I went into full-time ministry. Those early jobs were not happy activities for me, and at times, they were physically and emotionally painful; however, the way my father "disciplined" me played a vital role in many of the good things my heavenly Father wanted to do in my life and ministry.

As a good Father, God brings us into a wilderness in order to discipline us. Why is He so interested in our discipline? It is not because He seeks to punish us, nor is it that He is disappointed in us as His children or that He wishes we were better people. It is because He is preparing us for the promised land. In Deuteronomy 8:7, He told the Hebrews why He was disciplining them: *"For the Lord your God is bringing you into a good land, a land of brooks of water, of fountains and springs, flowing forth in valleys and hills."* In every wilderness we face, we can rest confident in this fact: God's heart is to do good for us in the end.[4] We can conclude that our loving Father in Heaven is working to give us good gifts, in every moment, in every wilderness. Those good gifts are closely tied to our unique destinies and purposes for living on this earth.

God Will Not Abandon Us

God will never abandon us in the wilderness or in any other season of life. That is the third important truth we need to remember when we are in a dry season. We don't experience difficulty because God is unconcerned about us. No, God is very concerned for our welfare—so much so that He is the One who actually leads us into the wilderness:

> *"Then Jesus was led up by the Spirit into the wilderness."*
> — Matthew 4:1

> *"You shall remember all the way which the Lord your God has led you in the wilderness these forty years."*
> — Deuteronomy 8:2

> *"He led you through the great and terrible wilderness."*
> — Deuteronomy 8:15

In all three of these passages, the Lord was leading the people He loved. He did not leave them alone in their times of trial—a wilderness is not a place of abandonment. Think about God's people in the Old Testament and how they treated Him. Even though the children of Israel were a rebellious, idolatrous, and sinful people, the Lord did not forsake them in the wilderness. He still led them and cared for them during that time. Nehemiah 9:19 sums everything up: *"You, in Your great compassion, did not forsake them in the wilderness."*

When we find ourselves in a wilderness, it is important for us to remember that our heavenly Father loves us. He will not abandon us, nor will He forsake us.[5] On the contrary, He is bringing us into destiny and purpose.

God Provides for Us

In a wilderness, the Lord will take care of us. Look at all the provisions He gave Israel in the desert:

1. He fed them with manna.

"Then the Lord said to Moses, 'Behold, I will rain bread from heaven for you; and the people shall go out and gather a day's portion every day, that I may test them, whether or not they will walk in My instruction.'" — Exodus 16:4

2. He gave them meat.

"Moses said, 'This will happen when the Lord gives you meat to eat in the evening, and bread to the full in the morning; for the Lord hears your grumblings which you grumble against Him. And what are we? Your grumblings are not against us but against the Lord.'" — Exodus 16:8

3. He gave them water to drink.

"He humbled you and let you be hungry, and fed you with manna which you did not know, nor did your fathers know, that He might make you understand that man does not live by bread alone, but man lives by everything that proceeds out of the mouth of the Lord." — Deuteronomy 8:3

4. He took care of their shoes and clothing.

"I have led you forty years in the wilderness; your clothes have not worn out on you, and your sandal has not worn out on your foot." — Deuteronomy 29:5

5. He took care of their physical bodies.

"Your clothing did not wear out on you, nor did your foot swell these forty years." — Deuteronomy 8:4

6. He gave them a cloud to shelter them by day and a pillar of fire by night.

"And with a pillar of cloud You led them by day, And with a pillar of fire by night To light for them the way In which they were to go." — Nehemiah 9:12

7. He protected them.

"But Moses said to the people, 'Do not fear! Stand by and see the salvation of the Lord which He will accomplish for you today; for the Egyptians whom you have seen today, you will never see them again forever. The Lord will fight for you while you keep silent.'" — Exodus 14:13–14

God met every need Israel had. Think about it — they essentially had "room service" for forty years! God gave them good clothes to wear and took care of their bodies. He provided air conditioning (the shadow of a cloud) by day and heat (the pillar of fire) by night. He protected them. In every way, God took care of them while they were in the wilderness. If He took care of the Hebrews during their trials, He will also take care of us. In all things He is our Provider.

When Paula and I were in the "seminary wilderness," God did so many precious miracles for us. Even though we didn't have the resources we had before, what we did have became invaluable revelations of God's love and care for us. The revelation of God's love and care is the summary of what a wilderness looks like. When we are smack dab in the midst of it, it can be hard — but it isn't a time of abandonment. In fact, the fruit of a wilderness can be beautiful.

God Gives Fresh Words for New Seasons

"Therefore, behold, I will allure her, Bring her into the wilderness And speak kindly to her." — Hosea 2:14

The fifth truth we need to remember in the wilderness is that God's Word is present for us. The importance we place on God's Word in a wilderness sets our level of stability or instability. His Word is true and real and applies to our lives right now, even in the midst of a wilderness. It will sustain us and help us. The revelation of that truth empowers us to face any adversity the world could send our way.

In a wilderness, what does it look like to be dependent on God's Word? Usually, it looks like two things. It could mean focusing on something God taught or showed us in the past, or it could mean new revelation for a new season. Many times in the wilderness, God will give us new understanding of His nature, character, and ways. These new revelations are like kisses from God to strengthen, empower, and sustain us.[6]

It is always good to receive fresh revelation of God's Word. The key is learning to be open to fresh unveilings of Him, while not drifting from the revelations He gave in the past.[7] That is an important skill to develop. Jesus said that *"every scribe who has become a disciple of the kingdom of heaven is like a head of a household, who brings out of his treasure things new and old"* (Matthew 13:52). In either situation, whether we are leaning on the beautiful truths God gave us in the past or hearing fresh revelation from His mouth, dependency on His words is crucial.

While Jesus was in the wilderness for forty days, He rested in God's Word. The enemy pushed against Him, but Jesus relied on the reality and power of words His Father had spoken in the past:

> *"But He answered and said, 'It is written, "Man shall not live on bread alone, but on every word that proceeds out of the mouth of God."'"* — Matthew 4:4

> *"Jesus said to him, 'On the other hand, it is written, "You shall not put the Lord your God to the test."'"* — Matthew 4:7

> *"Then Jesus said to him, 'Go, Satan! For it is written, "You shall worship the Lord your God, and serve Him only."'"* — Matthew 4:10

Three times in Matthew 4 Jesus declared, "It is written." He was using the Word to sustain Himself. Jesus was drawing the "past words" of God into His present situation.

Likewise, when David was in the wilderness, God embedded fresh revelation of His character in David's heart:

"Because Your lovingkindness is better than life,
My lips will praise You . . .
When I remember You on my bed,
I meditate on You in the night watches,
For You have been my help,
And in the shadow of Your wings I sing for joy."
— Psalm 63:3–7

God's Word, as it pertains to His character, sustained David when he was in the wilderness. He fed his soul on revelations of God. Personally, I believe his ability to depend on God's Word was established during this wilderness season. It empowered him to become king and a man after God's heart.[8]

Learning to feed and be satisfied on the "manna" of God's Word is one of the most important character traits we can acquire. If it isn't part of our character, we become thirsty and hungry when the lack of this world starts to draw on our souls, which causes us to try to satisfy ourselves with things of the world instead of God. It is in seasons of uncertainty when our souls learn how to be satisfied with Jesus' fullness.

God's Word is relevant, sustaining, satisfying, and fresh in every wilderness we face. If God has led us into a wilderness, we can rest assured that it will be a good thing.

In summary, God is always good, and He always gives good gifts. He won't leave or abandon us. He will take care of our every need. He will speak fresh revelation to us, or He will give an opportunity for the truths we heard in the past to be established in the depths of our hearts.

Notes / Reference Scriptures

1. Deueronomy 8:3
2. Psalm 73
3. Hebrews 12:5-13
4. Deuteronomy 8:16
5. Hebrews 13:5-6
6. Song of Solomon 1:2
7. Hebrews 2:1-3
8. Acts 13:22

2 The Characteristics of a Wilderness

A key to extracting everything we can from a wilderness experience is recognizing when we are in one and knowing what to expect from it. When we realize we are in a wilderness, we can direct our thoughts in a healthy way and actually take advantage of the situation to walk in victory.

The children of Israel didn't understand how a wilderness works. After crossing the Red Sea, they expected to immediately enter the Promised Land. Instead, they found themselves in a wilderness. They didn't know what God was doing, and they became frightened:

> *"Then Moses led Israel from the Red Sea, and they went out into the wilderness of Shur; and they went three days in the wilderness and found no water . . . So the people grumbled at Moses, saying, 'What shall we drink?'"*
> — Exodus 15:22–24

If we don't understand what is going on, we could end up doing what the Israelites did: panicking, losing trust in God, and giving up. We need to understand how a wilderness works and what to expect in a wilderness so we aren't taken by surprise.

First, let's look at what God is doing when He leads us into a wilderness.

A Wilderness Is a Season of Humility

"You shall remember all the way which the Lord your God has led you in the wilderness these forty years, that He might humble you." — Deuteronomy 8:2

In the wilderness, we are set free from pride. Our abilities, perceptions, and regular sources of provision are no longer present for us, or simply will not work, so we are compelled to lose our independent hearts and lay aside the pride that makes us think we are better than others. We begin to see God as He is: the Creator and Sustainer of all things. He is the One who provides for us. All good things come from Him, and we can possess only what comes from Him.[1] As we begin to understand that every good thing we have is a gift from the heart and hand of God — that is a revelation that leads to life.

No matter the length of the wilderness, whether it lasts for a single afternoon or several months, it instills within us a deep dependence on God because we don't have anyone or anything else to rely on. Therefore, humility is one of the main elements of a wilderness. Humility is from the Greek word tapeinos, which means "laying low." The way I see it, humility involves two elements in God's Word: dependency and perspective. As we put those two elements together, humility comes to mean seeing ourselves in a proper perspective to God and others and being totally dependent on God, His body, and His provision.

Humility is powerful. Numerous times in God's Word, exaltation is the result of humility. From a humble position, we are exalted into destiny. Three times in Deuteronomy 8 God emphasized that the purpose of the wilderness was to establish a humble heart in His people:

*"You shall remember all the way which the Lord your God has led you in the wilderness these forty years, that **He might humble you**, testing you, to know what was in your heart, whether you would keep His commandments or not. **He humbled you** and let you be hungry, and fed you with manna which you did not know, nor did your fathers know,*

that He might make you understand that man does not live by bread alone, but man lives by everything that proceeds out of the mouth of the Lord."
— Deuteronomy 8:2–3 (emphasis added)

*"In the wilderness He fed you manna which your fathers did not know, that **He might humble you** and that He might test you, to do good for you in the end."*
— Deuteronomy 8:16 (emphasis added)

Humility means having a right perspective that declares the Lord is God Most High. He is the Possessor of Heaven and earth, and all life and provision come from Him. Therefore, the end result of humility is dependency on God. We are set free from mindsets that tell us we have to do something. When we come out of the wilderness and enter the promised land, we have hearts that look forward to what God is going to do, not to winning our own glory. As we walk in the character of the Lord, obediently responding to His voice and living dependent on Him, He will bless the work of our hands.[2]

In seminary, my wilderness experience developed within me a mindset of dependency on God through prayer. After seminary, the staff, church members, and I prayed every weekday morning at the church from six to seven and every Saturday night at nine for the Sunday morning worship service. The result was a time of revival for our little Baptist church. I knew I didn't know what to do, so I depended on God to move. The only time I got in trouble was when I started thinking I knew something and forgot the revelation of humility I had learned during seminary.

A Wilderness Is a Season of Insecurity

"He led you through the great and terrible wilderness, with its fiery serpents and scorpions and thirsty ground where there was no water; He brought water for you out of the rock of flint."
— Deuteronomy 8:15

In a wilderness, it is common to feel insecure. We feel this way because we are confronted by overwhelming obstacles and threats that seem greater than we can handle. We often feel intimidated and helpless as we see obstacles we cannot conquer with our own resources. So a wilderness can be an opportunity for us to shed the belief that our resources are our source of security, and instead, we can discover the power and protection of the Lord.

All the fullness of God has been placed in Jesus—He is purposed to be the filler of all creation.[3] We can find our completeness only in Him. Because Jesus Christ is the filler of everything, when He fills our beings, we do not lack. When He is in me and I am in Him, all the fullness of God dwells in me. That is why John declared, *"Greater is He who is in you than he who is in the world"* (1 John 4:4). He is the One who satisfies every desire and brings security to our souls.

Overseas ministry trips are usually wilderness experiences for me because I am often confronted with circumstances I cannot handle on my own. These times are opportunities for me to discover the bigness of God. In my normal comfort zones of home, I can become complacent about resting in the Lord as my security, but in the wilderness far from home, I am able to receive the reality of God in the doubting areas of my heart.

The wilderness brings us back to our only lasting Source of security: Jesus. Every source of security offered by the world is temporary and will eventually leave us dry and empty. Once these sources of temporary security are put in order, we can receive the true security found in Christ.

A Wilderness Is a Season of the Unknown

"[He] fed you with manna which you did not know, nor did your fathers know." — Deuteronomy 8:3

The people of Israel didn't even know the food they were eating—they were clearly on a journey into the unknown. The wilderness can be like a heavenly Twilight Zone, where God works within us to bring us into new levels of faith. Faith is the assurance of things hoped for and the evidence of things not seen.[4] He empowers us to let go of the known and reach out with Him to grab the unknown.

It is amazing how humanity uses foods, smells, sights, and relationships as sources of confidence and security. Known things can bring us great comfort, but it is possible for those things to become forms of idolatry. In our hearts, we can set up a person, place, or thing as our source of strength and security, relying on that thing instead of Jesus. In the wilderness, the Lord will often take care of us with provisions and resources that are totally unfamiliar. When we are surrounded by unknown territory in a wilderness, we have to believe God's Word and trust His character.

During ministry trips overseas, the students in our school of ministry have a tendency to drift toward places and things that are familiar to them, like a McDonald's. The people who hardly ever eat at McDonald's in the United States look for a McDonald's overseas because it is something they recognize. A few years ago, we had two young ladies go on an overseas trip by themselves. As their hearts began to crave the familiar, they would sit for hours in front of a computer watching Animal Planet and eating animal crackers, because they were so homesick.

All of us have a tendency to look for the familiar to bring stability to our souls. But in a wilderness, we have an opportunity to experience the unknown.

A Wilderness Is a Season of Exposure

"And after He had fasted forty days and forty nights, He then became hungry." — Matthew 4:2

A wilderness is a place of exposure[5] where we feel vulnerable to people and elements around us.

God desires to meet all our needs so that our existence is never threatened. His heart is for us to walk in a state of perfect contentment. When we are filled with His fullness, nine characteristics of the Father are expressed and released in our lives:

love, acceptance, worth, intimacy, purpose, security, need to be needed, forgiveness, and identity. When those needs are met in God, we are able to walk in contentment. However, when events arise that threaten our existence, and our hearts are not secure in God and filled with His life, we launch a desperate struggle to find alternative sources of life—we look for ways to protect ourselves. As our hope and faith are distracted from God's truth, we are tempted to have our needs met in other things. We try to prove ourselves. We get intimidated. We become confused about who we are and what we want in life. Whenever instability occurs, our lives will be "out of control" on a soulish level, and we will have nothing firm and permanent on which we can fix our hearts and minds. Every wilderness, no matter its length, type, or nature, is a season in which our soulish needs are exposed. A soulish need is something our hearts and minds require in order to function in a healthy way.

The devil seeks to expose our needs in ways that will lead to massive soulish instability. Yet God lovingly works to reveal our needs in a slow and safe manner, so we can find our fullness in Christ. When Jesus' fullness is established in our hearts, all our needs are met—that is, His fullness satisfies all our needs. We are content. We have peace. Our minds are free to focus on things that are more important than our needs.

As a side note on this topic, whenever our physical needs are exposed, it reveals the source we are using to satisfy our soulish needs, which then reveals the source we are using to meet our spiritual needs. For example, if we realize we have no food in the cabinets and no money to buy more food, the environment of a physical need can reveal what we have been using to satisfy our souls. Where will we turn when the need is exposed? Are we trusting in God to meet all our needs, as His Word says He will do, or will we start worrying? The physical need exposes the source we have been using to meet our soulish needs. This, in turn, shows the source we are using to meet our spiritual needs.[A]

A Wilderness Is a Season of Uncertainty

"Therefore, behold, I will hedge up her way with thorns,
And I will build a wall against her so that she cannot find
her paths." — Hosea 2:6

Notice the phrase God used in Hosea 2: "She cannot find her paths." In a wilderness, our normal way of doing something—that is, the "path" we usually take—no longer works. It feels like we don't know where we are going or how to get where we need to go.

Imagine you are an Israelite who recently left Egypt. You have seen God perform miracle after miracle. You crossed the Red Sea and rejoiced when He saved you from your enemies. In this moment, everything seems certain; you know you can trust God to lead you. But then something happens. You expect the Promised Land, and you don't get it! Instead, you get a wilderness. You and your people wander the desert for a significant number of years, not days. What's going on?

Can you imagine the feeling of uncertainty involved in a situation like that? Some of us are good with taking our time and not having a clear plan. Others declare, "We have to know where we're going. We have to have a plan, and then we have to get there within the desired time frame." In a wilderness, that second attitude won't work because one of the main elements of this season is uncertainty. The plans we make seem to dissolve in smoke, and we don't always end up where we think we want to be.

I often tell the people who travel overseas with me, "Be flexible and cool." I am warning them that anytime we go into a "ministry wilderness," uncertainty is a common theme. Yet in times of uncertainty, we can learn to see God in new ways. The very foundations of our hearts are established in Him.

A Wilderness Is a Season of No Human Props

*"She will pursue her lovers, but she will not overtake them;
And she will seek them, but will not find them."*

— Hosea 2:7

I have described a wilderness as a place of humility, insecurity, the unknown, exposure, and uncertainty. We often feel these characteristics as strong emotions because in the wilderness we lose our human props. A prop describes something temporary.

In Scripture, the Lord uses words like trust, lean on,[6] and rely on[7] to describe our dependency on Him. The same words can also be used to describe how we can set up people, places, and things as sources of life. We can trust the world. We can lean and rely on the world. In a wilderness, our props are removed. Gomer wasn't able to find her counterfeit lovers in Hosea 2:7, which is a key characteristic of a wilderness. When the "prop" of her lovers was cut off, she panicked and in desperation turned to the Lord. It works in a similar way with each of us. When the worldly things we have used to satisfy our needs are suddenly no longer present or simply don't satisfy us anymore, we have the opportunity to make the Lord our Source.

A Wilderness Is a Season of Temptation

"Then Jesus was led up by the Spirit into the wilderness to be tempted by the devil." — Matthew 4:1

In a wilderness, we can expect the enemy to tempt us to sin, compromise, or take the quick and easy way out. (We will discuss this wilderness element more fully in later sections.)

God in the Wilderness

We can expect to experience seven characteristics in any wilderness we face: It is a season of humility, insecurity, the unknown, vulnerability, uncertainty, no human props, and temptation. It may be a scary-sounding list, but if we keep these characteristics in mind whenever we (or someone we love) are in a wilderness, we will be able to identify the season and extract its purpose. Knowing we are in a wilderness season will help us see the road a little more clearly. God doesn't want a wilderness to be a negative experience. Instead, He wants it to propel us into the promised land He has prepared for us—the very thing He told us to expect.

Notes / Reference Scriptures

A. To learn more about our physical, soulish, and spiritual needs, I recommend my book entitled - *Jesus: The Filler of Needs*. Visit dealingjesus.org for more information.

1. 1 Chronicles 29:14
2. Deuteronomy 8:16-18
3. Colossians 1:19
4. Hebrews 11:1
5. Hosea 2:3
6. Proverbs 3:5
7. Isaiah 10:20

3   The Four Areas of a Wilderness

We can experience a wilderness in at least four different areas of our lives. Each type of wilderness has a similar effect on our souls, and God's heart in each type is consistent — He wants to bring about life within us.

The wilderness, or dark night of the soul, is not just a theoretical concept to me. Having experienced all four wildernesses found in Scripture, I bear witness of the power and faithfulness of God to lead us through these seasons into the destinies He has for us.

Types of Wildernesses

Physical Wilderness

I experience a physical wilderness almost every time I travel overseas. This was particularly true in 1991 when I traveled to communist Cuba. I became very sick because of dumbness on my part, and two things made the situation even more difficult. For one, it was the first time I had ever been on a foreign mission trip, and secondly, I had failed to remember that I couldn't communicate with the United States because of the separation between the U.S. and Cuban governments. I was completely disconnected and alienated from my normal support systems, and I felt helpless. However, the Lord was faithful in His power to heal and in His presence to comfort.

Relational Wilderness

Many years ago, I left a ministry and went back to a church I loved, but it wasn't at the direction of God. I realize now I was struggling with an unhealthy need for relationships, and as a result, I entered a relational wilderness that lasted a couple of years. I remember telling close friends in the church that it didn't matter how hard things might be if I came back; as long as we had each other, it would be all right. But one by one, the relationships I had longed for dropped out of my life. I found myself completely submerged in a wilderness. It was one of the hardest, loneliest times of my life, but in the end, I was able to reestablish the relationship that is foundational and most important, which is, of course, my relationship with the Lord.

Economic Wilderness

Paula and I once bought a piece of property where we could build a retreat center. I was planning on using the sale of some business assets to help with the purchase, and when the business sales unexpectedly fell through, I found myself in an economic wilderness. During that time, I discovered two very important things. First, I realized the degree to which the love of money was permeating my heart, and the Lord helped me gain victory over it. Second, I realized the Lord's faithfulness to redeem and restore the situations that were causing the economic wilderness. Looking back, I would not take any amount of money in exchange for the things the Lord did in me when those business deals fell through.

Wilderness of Purpose

When Paula and I moved to Boone, North Carolina, God began to fulfill the purposes of my family; He poured out tremendous blessings on Paula and the kids, and they were able to do the things He had created them to do. But for me, that season in Boone was a wilderness of purpose. I wasn't sure of the call of God on my life and didn't know how to move forward. In the midst of my uncertainty, I had to rely on God more than ever, and as I did, He began to birth the fullness of His purpose for me. It was not easy—but I learned how He wanted me to live. I learned what real life looks like.

Our Father wants us to come to rely on Him and know Him in greater ways. Anytime we talk about the wilderness, we need to remember that if anything is important to us, it is important to God. Let's look at each of these four wilderness experiences more closely.

The Physical Wilderness

When Jesus was in the wilderness, right after His baptism, the situation was completely different than anything He had ever encountered. Some thirty years earlier, He was with the Father, saturated with the fullness of God.[1] But in the wilderness, there was nothing in His physical reality that Jesus could use as a source of comfort.

I would call what Jesus encountered a physical wilderness. This type of wilderness occurs when we are outside our comfort zones physically speaking and are separated from what we consider to be "normal." As I mentioned earlier, when I travel overseas I often find myself in a type of physical wilderness. The food is different, the toilets are different, and the showers are different. The people look and sound different, and even the smells are different. Those things may sound mundane, but being in a completely different culture can easily reveal our hearts and the sources we are relying on for fulfillment.

A physical wilderness is anything that causes us to experience some level of physical discomfort; it could be something as simple as a fast or a lack of sleep. When our bodies are hungry or tired but we choose not to satisfy those needs, we give God a huge opportunity to work in our hearts. We are forcing our physical bodies not to use food or sleep as a means of comfort. Is a lack of hunger the only reason we are walking in the Spirit? Is being well rested the only reason we are following the Spirit's leading?

Don't tell them this, but sometimes when we send our students on ministry trips, we purposely schedule travel times so the students will have only a small amount of sleep. This is part of their training; we do this so they can learn to lean on the Spirit of God when they are weak. A lack of sleep or feeling hungry is not an excuse for being grouchy. In a physical wilderness, we can allow our hearts to be established in the Lord and develop dependency on His Holy Spirit.

A physical wilderness affects the stability of our souls. It was after Jesus had fasted for forty days, when He was physically hungry, that the devil came to tempt Him. When we are in a vulnerable spot physically, our souls can start to feel vulnerable as well, and in this type of wilderness, the Lord is usually working in our hearts to establish our identity and security in Him. What better time to challenge our identity than when we are outside our culture? Outside our boundaries of "homeland," people have different ways of thinking and different things to think about. We might not have anything in common with them, but when our identity is established in Christ Jesus, who makes no distinction between any race,[2] it is possible for us to be comfortable with all people, no matter their race, creed, or color.

Finally, a physical wilderness also affects the security of our souls. When we feel vulnerable and exposed, we can direct our hearts into the secret place of God's presence.[3] We can allow our hearts to be established in His name — that is, in His nature and character.[4] There, we rediscover who the Lord is and find that He is strong and mighty in battle.

The Relational Wilderness

In a relational wilderness, the relationships that used to be a source of equilibrium for us are no longer present. A relational wilderness is any season in which we have lost loved ones through death, betrayal, desertion, personal isolation, or by a change in location.

David was in a relational wilderness when he hid in the cave of Adullam:

> *"So David departed from there and escaped to the cave of Adullam; and when his brothers and all his father's household heard of it, they went down there to him. Everyone who was in distress, and everyone who was in debt, and everyone who was discontented gathered to him; and he became captain over them. Now there were about four hundred men with him."*   — 1 Samuel 22:1–2

Notice that the people with him were "in debt," "distressed," and "discontented." In other words, his companions weren't the healthy, strong pillars of society. They were in bad shape spiritually and emotionally. When we are going through hardship or have become familiar with difficulty, it is easy for us to grow bitter, negative, and distrusting. We see this same crew later in 1 Samuel 30:5–6, where the Bible says they were embittered against David. Their families had been kidnapped, which is a horrific difficulty; however, they wouldn't have been thinking about killing David if they had been completely happy with him before the kidnapping occurred. They must have been a little bitter and "discontented" already.

Going back to the cave of Adullam, when I see the reference to David's family, I cannot help but wonder what they were thinking. I can almost hear them berating David: "What are you doing down here with these people? You used to be in the king's court, and now look at you—what are you doing?"

For a season, none of David's relationships could give him

relational stability. In a sense, he was on his own. Psalm 142, which he wrote while living in a cave, reflects the relational wilderness he was experiencing:

> *"Look to the right and see;*
> *For there is no one who regards me;*
> *There is no escape for me;*
> *No one cares for my soul."*
> — Psalm 142:4

A common, more modern example of a relational wilderness is what single people go through as they hope to meet their spouses. I know a number of people who were single who had words from God concerning the people they were going to marry. In most of these cases, my single friends received this revelation and then experienced a season in which there was no one, anywhere, who seemed to confirm what God was saying. Instead of meeting their spouses right away, they ended up going through a dry time relationally.

We can also find ourselves in a relational wilderness when we have allowed relationships to become sources of idolatry; we can start to crave human relationships more than we long for the Lord. In this case, the important truth to remember is that the Lord will never leave us, nor will He ever forsake us.[5] He may be silent in these times, but He is still present because He will never violate His promise.

We see a relational wilderness in the Old Testament with King Hezekiah:

> *"Even in the matter of the envoys of the rulers of Babylon,*
> *who sent to him to inquire of the wonder that had happened*
> *in the land, God left him alone only to test him, that He*
> *might know all that was in his heart."*
> — 2 Chronicles 32:31

The Lord didn't leave Hezekiah permanently—only in this matter involving the envoys. Hezekiah allowed pride to enter his heart because God had blessed him with wealth and resources, and he started craving the relationships of the world.

So the Lord was silent in order that Hezekiah might realize he was prideful. Years later, Hezekiah's pride was the reason the Babylonians came to conquer Judah.

In Scripture, wells, cisterns, and springs are often metaphors for relationships. In the following passage, Israel had forsaken a relationship with the Lord and sought after other relationships they thought could hold or give life:

> *"For My people have committed two evils:*
> *They have forsaken Me,*
> *The fountain of living waters,*
> *To hew for themselves cisterns,*
> *Broken cisterns That can hold no water . . .*
> *Have you not done this to yourself*
> *By your forsaking the Lord your God*
> *When He led you in the way?*
> *But now what are you doing on the road to Egypt, To drink*
> *the waters of the Nile?*
> *Or what are you doing on the road to Assyria,*
> *To drink the waters of the Euphrates?*
> *Your own wickedness will correct you."*
> — Jeremiah 2:13,17–19

The Lord was essentially asking Israel, "Why do you want to go back to what you knew in the past?" Israel had lived in Egypt, and now they were on the "road to Egypt" to "drink the waters of the Nile." In other words, they were going back to relationships of the past—of the world. Similarly, traveling "the road to Assyria" to "drink the waters of the Euphrates" is symbolic of starting relationships of compromise and being unequally yoked with unbelievers.

When we start going back to past relationships or relationships that simply aren't the best for us, we might get what we want for a time. But those relationships don't generate life. They take life from us. As soon as we realize they are fruitless and it is the Lord we really want, He will quickly reveal Himself in order to comfort and sustain us with true life.

One of the great joys in my life was when my daughter, Michele, worked with me in the internship program in our church. However, those days were preceded by a painful wilderness that occurred as she finished community college and was about to transfer to another school to finish her degree. We moved her into a one-bedroom apartment, and I remember wanting to make sure she felt safe and comfortable, because she was going to be spending a lot of time by herself.

She began to get lonely. She attended a ministry on campus, but no one really reached out to her. To add fuel to the fire, she and a male friend were praying about starting a relationship, and the guy ended up calling things off. I called her often to encourage her. There were times when my heart so longed for her to have friendship that her mother and I, or just me by myself, would drive the two-and-a-half-hour trip to take her out to dinner and spend time with her. It was a lonely but profitable time. I watched my daughter mature into a precious woman of God. She went through that year faithfully, excelling in her schoolwork and drawing closer to the Lord. At the end of the school year, she talked to Paula and me and asked if she could come back to Virginia, attend Virginia Tech, and work with me in the internship program. I loved it. She traveled with me overseas and helped me minister the Gospel, and I knew a lot of the things she shared with our interns came out of that time when she was alone, when it was just her and the Lord.

God's Heart in the Relational Wilderness

The relational wilderness is a time when we are separated from all relationships except our relationship with the Lord (and possibly other critical relationships like those with a spouse and children). It is a time to discover the most important aspect of life: our relationship with God.

In a relational wilderness, the Lord is working to strengthen our hearts in the reality of His love, acceptance, and intimacy. Two things are happening in a relational wilderness. First, the Lord is strengthening our hearts so He can be our focus and the filler of our needs of love and acceptance. Second, the Lord is transitioning us into a place of ministry, where we will be able to help other people direct their hearts toward Lord.

The Economic Wilderness

An economic wilderness occurs when a person's financial welfare enters a season of uncertainty. It isn't always a time of financial crisis, but our finances can get pretty lean, and we just don't have enough resources to be able to enjoy life.[6]

A financial wilderness is a time of financial humility:

> *"In the wilderness He fed you manna which your fathers did not know, that He might humble you and that He might test you, to do good for you in the end. Otherwise, you may say in your heart, 'My power and the strength of my hand made me this wealth.'"*
>
> — Deuteronomy 8:16–17

In an economic wilderness, we come to understand it is the Lord who will supply all our needs. During this season, we often have financial provision in ways we don't understand. "How did this happen? How is it that we have enough toilet paper and food in the cupboards? How is it that we paid the bills but have money left over? I don't get it." It is like getting water out of a rock or having bread fall from Heaven—it isn't what you expect.

When Paula and I left everything we knew to go into full-time ministry, things didn't work out exactly as we had planned. Our finances dropped off a cliff. We went from eating out at fine restaurants as often as we wanted to buying ninety-nine-cent hamburgers once a week. Our living conditions downsized to a very small apartment. We had enough to pay our bills, and that was pretty much the end of the story where our money was concerned. Yet during that season, whenever an unexpected crisis occurred, the Lord would send what we needed in some of the most unexpected ways. As an example, when our car broke down, the exact money we needed to pay for the repair came in the mail the same day. God was so faithful, and we learned so much during that time about the true meaning of life and resources.

The Wilderness of Purpose

In a wilderness of purpose, nothing in our lives seems to support or confirm what we are called to do. Abraham experienced an intense wilderness of purpose. God told him he was going to be a father of many nations, but He said this at a time when Abraham's wife, Sarah, was barren.[7] There was no "proof" in Abraham's life to confirm God's word to him.

Years later, God told Joseph he was going to be a powerful ruler—but that wasn't what immediately happened. Instead, Joseph was sold into slavery and later thrown into prison. Nothing in Joseph's life seemed to confirm the purpose God had given him. In fact, by all appearances he was moving away from the possibility of his purpose being fulfilled. A wilderness of purpose is a season in which we cannot see how our circumstances and God's promise will ever come into agreement. We don't know what is going on, and life feels uncertain, unpredictable, and unsafe.

As I mentioned earlier, Paula and I had a difficult time when we entered seminary, and that difficulty extended beyond our finances. As a whole, it was a very dry time, and I had only a handful of ministry opportunities. It became so bad that one day while Paula was watching a video of me preaching, she asked the Lord, "Are You sure Rick is called to preach?" We were giving it our all and not seeing much fruit. I knew God had called me to minister the Gospel to the nations, but it seemed like that wasn't happening.

A wilderness of purpose is a time of barrenness and uncertainty regarding God's purposes for our lives. But a wilderness of purpose is also an opportunity for us to realize the Lord is our purpose. So many times we come to the Lord wanting to know the answers to life's questions: Who am I going to marry? What kind of job am I going to have? What is my calling? We can become so obsessed with discovering the plans He has for us that we miss living life with Him right now.

Jeremiah 29:11–14 shows us what God is looking for:

> *"'For I know the plans that I have for you,' declares the Lord, 'plans for welfare and not for calamity to give you a future and a hope. Then you will call upon Me and come and pray to Me, and I will listen to you. You will seek Me and find Me when you search for Me with all your heart. I will be found by you,' declares the Lord, 'and I will restore your fortunes and will gather you from all the nations and from all the places where I have driven you,' declares the Lord, 'and I will bring you back to the place from where I sent you into exile.'"*

Verse 11 is all about plans. Following a natural progression, the next verses should tell us how to discover those plans, but instead, the next verses are all about discovering the Lord. The pinnacle of the passage is that when we search for the Lord with all our hearts, we will find the Lord—and when we have the Lord, we have a plan and a purpose.

It was in the wilderness that Abraham, who was destined to become the father of our faith, discovered how to live by faith. It was in the wilderness that Joseph discovered that his purpose was not the most important thing. The most important thing was the process and heart of the purpose. He learned to love his brothers and not boast of his God-given destiny. In these times of difficulty, God was faithful to reveal Himself and the purposes He had for His people. The biggest revelation we could grasp is that the Lord is our purpose.

The wilderness of purpose is that season when we discover the awesomeness of God, His timing, and His procedures for walking in the paths He has for us.

God in the Wilderness

In summary, we can experience a wilderness in at least four different areas of our lives: physically, relationally, financially, and concerning our purpose. Each of these seasons is designed to empower us to go into our promised land.

Whenever we face a wilderness, the most important thing we need to remember is that God promised to walk with us. He will never leave us. Most of us tend to go into a mild panic when we think we could be entering a wilderness; however, it is possible to face these seasons with confidence.

We need to gain a proper perspective of our heavenly Father. He is not trying to hurt us or punish us. In a season of wilderness, He is working to bring us out of negative, painful mindsets, like that of an orphan, slave, or immature child, so we can walk in His freedom. A wilderness is a very important part of our spiritual development.

When we understand the Lord and how He uses the wilderness, we will see a loving Father trying to position us for success and life. In the next chapter, we are going to take a closer look at the purposes of a wilderness.

Notes / Reference Scriptures

1. John 17:5
2. Colossians 3:11
3. Psalms 27:5; 91:1-4
4. Proverbs 18:10
5. Hebrews 13:5-6
6. 1 Timothy 6:17
7. Genesis 11:30

Why Am I Here? Reasons for the Wilderness

Two precious friends of mine, Robbie and Toni, left their positions at a successful ministry in Florida and moved up to Virginia to start a drug and alcohol regeneration program. But when they arrived, there was nothing for them to do. Robbie got a job painting houses and gradually became discouraged. Every ministry he tried to join ended up not working out. Eventually, he started his own painting business in order to take care of his family, and numerous times he almost quit and went back to Florida and the ministry they had left. He even had an offer to go back and be a worship leader with a dear friend he had worked with before. The wilderness seemed like it would never end.

But God was doing a work in Robbie and Toni. One day at a point of desperation, Robbie cried out to the Lord, who revealed that painting would be a part of his ministry. Not long after that, a man named Adam started coming to our church, and he needed help getting set free from substance abuse. He and another single brother moved into an apartment together, and that was the beginning of Eagle's Nest Regeneration Program. Today the ministry is partially funded by a painting business that has become one of the largest paint purchasers in our region.

Robbie and Toni were in the middle of a wilderness of purpose when God launched them into their ministry. In the midst of the wilderness, Robbie learned how to run a paint business and how to walk as a man of God outside the structure of his previous ministry. He and Toni learned so many things during that season that enabled the Eagle's Nest to become what it is today. Now at any given time you can find more than thirty men living and working together as their lives and the lives of their families are changed by the power of God. Numerous lives have been saved and redeemed through the power of the Gospel of Jesus Christ flowing through this ministry.

The main thing Robbie and Toni discovered during this time was that the Lord does the work, and He is the fulfiller of their purpose. Those wilderness years were not easy for them, but the fruit of that wilderness is affecting lives for eternity.

God is always working to bring an eternal blessing into our lives. He does not randomly lead us into a wilderness. There is a purpose in everything He does: "We know that God causes all things to work together for good to those who love God, to those who are called according to His purpose" (Romans 8:28). Our Father sews the tapestry of our lives into something beautiful and good. In every circumstance and in every season, God is working to bring us good.

From God's perspective, a wilderness is a doorway for good to be birthed and released in our lives. Sometimes in our twenty-first-century Christianity, we look for the short-term comfort and fulfillment, and yes, these things matter to God, but He is eternal. He wants to bring about eternal glory and blessing. The apostle Paul wrote, *"For I consider that the sufferings of this present time are not worthy to be compared with the glory that is to be revealed to us"* (Romans 8:18). In the wilderness, the Lord is working to see Heaven's blessings released in our lives. Said another way, He wants to release on the earth His Kingdom and His will that exists in Heaven.

We can clearly see God's desire in Israel's story. We talked about how He led Israel out of Egypt and straight into a wilderness. They were in the desert for three months before He took them to Mount Sinai, the mountain of God, and there, in the wilderness at the foot of the mountain, Israel received fresh revelation of God's ways and His law. After that radical encounter, He took them into the wilderness again so they could learn to fight. He wanted them to be men of war, who were valiant and capable of great deeds; they were not slaves any longer and could not continue to think like slaves. When the time had come, He brought them to Kadesh-barnea, where they sent out spies to bring back a report about the Promised Land, the rich country God had given them. In each of these steps in the wilderness, God was doing a work in and for His people, a work for their good, and He is doing the same in our lives.

Being Prepared for the Promised Land

The principal reason God leads us into a wilderness is to prepare us for our promised land. He is a Father. As such, He doesn't do anything that would harm His children; the wilderness is one of the ways He seeks to prepare us for the blessings and challenges of life.[1] In order to thrive in the wilderness, we have to know in our hearts that God is not trying to hurt us. He is trying to teach us how to live in a state of blessing.

My daughter, Michele, studied equine science at Virginia Tech. She has loved horses ever since she was little and wanted a pickup truck so she could pull a horse trailer. As her father, I want to see Michele's dreams come to pass. That is my heart for her. Let's say that having a pickup is part of her destiny. If I, as her dad, gave her that part of her destiny before she was ready, I could bring great harm to her. A twelve-year-old doesn't know how to drive, and she could hurt herself or destroy the truck. So the best thing I could do for her is prepare her beforehand and teach her how to drive and take care of a vehicle. God created us for a purpose, according to His plan.[2] As a loving Father, He desires to see us fulfill that purpose. If He brings us into the "promised lands" of our lives before we can handle them, they could destroy us or we could destroy the land.

A wilderness is one of the main tools God uses to bring us into the fullness of what He promised. God told Moses the end result of Israel's wilderness experience — it was so they would be able to live in godliness and blessing in the Promised Land:

"All the commandments that I am commanding you today you shall be careful to do, that you may live and multiply, and go in and possess the land which the Lord swore to give to your forefathers. You shall remember all the way which the Lord your God has led you in the wilderness these forty years, that He might humble you, testing you, to know what was in your heart, whether you would keep His command-ments or not." — Deuteronomy 8:1–2

The people were about to come into extreme abundance. The land was flowing with provision,[3] and Israel needed to be prepared to handle the change. Receiving great resources quickly without preparation is incredibly dangerous for our souls. Proverbs 20:21 says that an *"inheritance gained hurriedly at the beginning will not be blessed in the end."* We see this in the number of people who win the lottery and then experience great upheaval in their lives, because they can't handle such a rapid increase in wealth. I once heard a friend say, "The great-est temptation that we can ever face is success." Over the years, I have realized again and again the truth of that declaration.

God in His great love for us will lead us into a wilderness to prepare us for the abundance of His great purposes. Each of us is called to walk in the fullness of His glory and goodness, and His goodness can be overwhelmingly good. If we are not prepared for it, it can actually destroy us.

Being Proven: The Method of Preparation

The main way God prepares us for His promises is through a process called being proven. The biblical meaning of the word proven is the same as tested. In other words, as we start to leave the wilderness experience behind, God seeks to test us.

We can see God's testing-proving process numerous times throughout Scripture:

With the Hebrews

*"Then [Moses] cried out to the Lord, and the Lord showed him a tree; and he threw it into the waters, and the waters became sweet. There He made for them a statute and regulation, and **there He tested them.**"*
                    — Exodus 15:25 (emphasis added)

*"Then the Lord said to Moses, 'Behold, I will rain bread from heaven for you; and the people shall go out and gather a day's portion every day, **that I may test them**, whether or not they will walk in My instruction.'"*
                    — Exodus 16:4 (emphasis added)

*"Moses said to the people, 'Do not be afraid; for God has come **in order to test** you, and in order that the fear of Him may remain with you, so that you may not sin.'"*
                    — Exodus 20:20 (emphasis added)

With Abraham

*"Now it came about after these things, that **God tested Abraham**, and said to him, 'Abraham!' And he said, 'Here I am.'"*   — Genesis 22:1 (emphasis added)

With Joseph

"They afflicted his feet with fetters,
He himself was laid in irons;
Until the time that his word came to pass,
***The word of the Lord tested him.**"*
                    — Psalm 105:18–19 (emphasis added)

With Hezekiah

*"Even in the matter of the envoys of the rulers of Babylon, who sent to him to inquire of the wonder that had happened in the land, **God left him alone only to test him**, that He might know all that was in his heart."*
                    — 2 Chronicles 32:31 (emphasis added)

With Jesus

*"Then Jesus was led up by the Spirit into the wilderness to be **tempted by the devil**."*
> — Matthew 4:1 (emphasis added)

With Peter

*"Simon, Simon, behold, Satan has demanded permission to **sift you like wheat**."* — Luke 22:31 (emphasis added)

As you can see, being proven — that is, being tested — is an important part of the wilderness experience. In every wilderness, it plays an intricate role in our receiving the promises God has for us. James 1:12 puts it this way: *"Blessed is a man who perseveres under trial; for once he has been approved [tested and proven], he will receive the crown of life which the Lord has promised to those who love Him."*

Most of us think of testing as a negative experience, but in actuality, it can be an extremely positive experience. The words that are translated "proven" or "tested" have basically three different applications in God's Word. When we look at these applications, we can see how a wilderness can prepare us for our promised land.

Refining or Purifying

The Hebrew word bahan means the "proving or testing of metals in fire." The hotter the metal, the more the impurities are revealed — and therefore can be removed. The more the gold is proven, the more valuable it becomes. Proverbs 17:3 says, *"The refining pot is for silver and the furnace for gold, but the Lord tests hearts."* When our hearts are proven, their contents become more glorious and honorable:

> *"So that the proof of your faith, being more precious than gold which is perishable, even though tested by fire, may be*

found to result in praise and glory and honor at the revelation of Jesus Christ."　　　　　— 1 Peter 1:7

The wilderness reveals our "impurities"—the worldly sources we have been using to meet our needs. The wilderness is actually doing us a favor—we want to have our needs met in Jesus. When we realize we are going somewhere else to have our needs met, we can adjust what should be adjusted and allow the Lord to be the One who meets our needs.

To Try Out or Practice With

The Hebrew word nasah literally means "to try out" or "to find out; examine for value, quality, or use." It is the word David used when he couldn't wear Saul's armor because he hadn't "tested" it.[4]

Nasah is similar to test-driving a car. We drive the vehicle to get a feel for it and see if we are interested in purchasing it. When we encounter a wilderness, we experience what it is like to allow the Lord to be the fulfiller and satisfier of our needs. In a manner of speaking, we are getting a "feel" for Him. We are learning about Him and coming to understand that He is as good as He says He is.

Able to Tell the Difference and Quality

The Greek word *dokimazo* literally means "to test, prove, discern, or distinguish."

"And do not be conformed to this world, but be transformed by the renewing of your mind, so that you may prove what the will of God is, that which is good and acceptable and perfect." — Romans 12:2 (see also Philippians 1:9–10)

Being proven in the wilderness empowers us to distinguish between good and bad. It is interesting to note that *dokimazo*, the New Testament word for "proven," includes the meaning and application of both *bahan* and *nasah*, the two previous Hebrew words. So being proven embraces three different facets of meaning. The first carries with it the ability to purify or refine. The second means to try out or "test drive" something, and the third meaning denotes the ability to discern between good and bad.

Times of testing aren't meant to be negative experiences. In the wilderness, our blinders are removed, and we start to see God in new ways. His promises begin to take root in our lives.

What Does Being Proven Do?

Every time He tests us, God is giving us the opportunity to have better lives than we had before. Just the potential outcomes of God's proving process make the process itself worth it.

What are the outcomes of being proven?

Motives of Our Hearts Are Revealed

> *"You shall remember all the way which the Lord your God has led you in the wilderness these forty years, that He might humble you, testing you, to know what was in your heart, whether you would keep His commandments or not."* — Deuteronomy 8:2

God is omniscient. He knows all things and sees all things; He already knows what is in our hearts. We are the ones who need to know the contents of our hearts.

God led Israel into the wilderness to expose how their hearts were "programmed." The programming of our hearts (our conclusions about life) determines what we do, hear, say, love, believe, and feel. When we know what is in our hearts, we can, by God's grace and mercy, allow His truth to change us where we need to be changed.[A]

Imagine being able to hook up a computer to your heart. You could punch a few buttons on the keyboard, and all your inner "programming" would appear on the screen, where you could sort through it, delete the files or programs you didn't want, and arrange different elements in order of importance. God uses a wilderness the way we would use a computer—the wilderness reveals our programming. How can we be transformed into Jesus' likeness if we don't see the "viruses," or lies, in our hearts? When these things are brought into the light, we can participate with God in His process of conforming us into Jesus' image. We can begin to change the way we think when we realize how we are thinking.

One of the main purposes of the proving process is to reveal the conclusions of our hearts.[5] It is *bahan*, the Hebrew word used for refining gold. As gold is heated and refined, the impurities are separated from the precious metal, and the gold is purified.

We Become Perfected

> *"Consider it all joy, my brethren, when you encounter various trials, knowing t hat the testing of your faith produces endurance. And let endurance have its perfect result, so that you may be perfect and complete, lacking in nothing."*
> — James 1:2–4

On the other side of the wilderness is a man or woman of God who is strong and can withstand the temptations of the enemy and the pressures of the world. Those who have been proven in the wilderness are able to rest in the fullness found in Jesus; they are untouched by anything that would try to get them off track.

When the Hebrew children came out of Egypt and entered the wilderness, they were unproven. They knew very little about the pressures of war and how to conquer territory. In particular, they didn't know how to fight. Most of the Hebrews were slaves in Egypt; all they knew how to do was serve. Those who had been slaves began to panic when they suddenly needed to live an "unseen" life of faith; they wanted to go back to Egypt, to what they had seen and known in the past. But the Hebrews who were born in the wilderness had a different story. They were able to live in faith, daring to believe God for great things. When they faced trials, they knew the Lord would take care of them.

A wilderness gives us the ability to live with God in a realm that is not bound by what is physically seen, heard, or felt. Remember how the children of Israel had never seen the provisions the Lord had provided for them in the wilderness.[6] The food was unlike anything they had ever eaten, and it came in a way they had never seen. Simply, they had to trust the Lord. They could not plan it out, work it out, or manipulate it. By faith, they had to trust in a supernatural, unseen Source.

A wilderness is the opportunity to learn to live by faith in God, not resting in what we see:

> *"Now faith is the assurance of things hoped for, the conviction of things not seen."* — Hebrews 11:1

> *"For we walk by faith, not by sight."*
> — 2 Corinthians 5:7

Paul wrote in 2 Corinthians 4:17–18 that the seen is temporary and the unseen is eternal. God is a spiritual being. He operates and exists in another realm and in another type of time — He is eternal. His spiritual realm impacts and dictates the occurrences of the physical realm.[7] We, too, are spiritual beings, living in physical, fleshly bodies. Humanity has a tendency to focus on fulfilling our short-term physical and soulish needs, which God does care about, yet His first purpose is to establish us eternally and spiritually. This means being established in the unseen.

God's heart is for us to be righteous men and women, who live and walk in faith: *"For in it the righteousness of God is revealed from faith to faith; as it is written, 'But the righteous man shall live by faith'"* (Romans 1:17). Being content in a wilderness is a matter of faith, living on the unknown sources of God.

When we are tested, we become perfect. The wilderness can establish within us endurance and strength to face hard times. When steel has been tested, it becomes tempered steel, which is much stronger, more flexible, and more enduring than steel that has not been tested by fire. In other words, the fire brings the steel to a perfect and complete state. In the "fire" of a wilderness, we become "flexible" enough to live by faith in times of uncertainty. Consider the men and women who faced the Great Depression and World War II; that generation tends to be strong and enduring, despite hard times. They have been tested in the fire, and the result is strength.

I remember when the perceived "horrors" of Y2K were about to hit, and the news outlets were predicting disaster because of outdated computer codes in important networking systems throughout the world. It was forecasted that our power, financial, and other crucial infrastructures would crash when the year transitioned from 1999 to 2000. My dad lived through the Great Depression and fought in World War II, and I asked him if he was concerned about Y2K, explaining there was a possibility we could lose all our services — online banking, computing, and many other modern conveniences. He replied that when he was growing up, they didn't have any of those things and they survived just fine. If he did it before, he could do it again. As the clock ticked into New Year's Day and the rest of us stayed up to see if anything would happen, my dad slept through the whole thing. He was totally unconcerned.

Those who have lived through the uncertainties of the wilderness are proven. In their hearts and minds, they know they can face the trials and temptations of success and failure. They are perfect and complete, lacking in nothing.

Our Character Becomes Known

> "We also exult in our tribulations, knowing that tribulation brings about perseverance; and perseverance, proven character; and **proven character**, hope; and hope does not disappoint, because the love of God has been poured out within our hearts through the Holy Spirit who was given to us."
> — Romans 5:3-5 (emphasis added)

When we have come through the trials of a wilderness, our hearts are known and safe. We know what it takes to stand in tough times. We have been proven, and now we can be trusted with the wealth and treasures of God.[8]

Regular glass can be dangerous when it breaks because it shatters in large pieces, and the larger the piece of broken glass, the greater the potential for serious injury. Tempered glass, however, has gone through a process of intense heat that causes the glass to break into tiny pieces instead of large ones. The small pieces are less likely to cause injury.

A process of "intense heat" has a similar effect on the children of God. As we walk through seasons of wilderness in faith, we become men and women who are healthy and can be entrusted with the mysteries of God. We are the stewards of those mysteries.[9]

In Deuteronomy 8:1, the Lord wanted Israel to go in and possess the rich, abundant land He had prepared for them. He desires the same for us, but this is the challenge: Will we be able to walk in complete dependency on the fullness of God's character, even in a time of blessing? The answer to that question determines whether or not we need to pass through a wilderness before we enter the promised land. God wants us to be able to live in a state of loving obedience even in the midst of abundant blessing.

Abraham was blessed in all he touched, and he became the father of many nations. His times in the wilderness prepared him for abundance and fatherhood. He faced the "wilderness" of his wife's barrenness[10] and the "wilderness" of famine in the Promised Land.[11] But in the midst of hardship, he was proven and established in God's promises, and he reached the Promised Land.

By the time Joseph became a ruler in Egypt, he was able to rest in God's character and nature despite massive blessings, for he had been proven in the wilderness. God gave him back his family. His brothers, who previously meant to harm him, came to him for help. Because the character of God was established in his heart, Joseph was able to bless freely and love those who had injured him in the past.

A number of years ago, I was with a friend at a car auction when I received a notice on my pager to call someone back in my hometown area. Using the nearest pay phone, I discovered the person trying to reach me was a young wife and mother in our church who began to tell me that she was attracted to me. I stood there speechless. I had ministered with her a few times, and she and her husband were friends of ours. In the end, I told her this was unacceptable and we would talk when I got back. That afternoon when I got back into town, I told my wife what had happened, and then I met with the elders of our church and told them. Paula and I went over to the woman's house to talk with her and her husband, and we ministered to them. The interesting thing was that through this event, the husband and I became even better friends. I realized he truly trusted me because of my response to the situation. In his mind, I was tested and proven faithful. Any time of testing can be tough, but the results are priceless. Our hearts are purified, and we become complete.

A Time to Learn Obedience

Another purpose the Lord emphasizes in the wilderness is obedience:

> *"Then the Lord said to Moses, 'Behold, I will rain bread from heaven for you; and the people shall go out and gather a day's portion every day, that I may test them, whether or not they will walk in My instruction.'"* — Exodus 16:4

One of the main purposes of a wilderness is to establish within us hearts and minds that are unconditionally obedient to the Lord. Is our obedience and love for the Lord dependent upon good things and good times, or are they unconditional? Do we love, obey, and believe He is a good God no matter the circumstances we find ourselves in, or are we allowing our circumstances to define who our heavenly Father is?

At our first pastorate, a precious little Baptist church in southwest Virginia, Paula had an experience that showed us the significance of obeying the Lord. An attractive woman about our age started attending the church. The woman was divorced, and she had a reputation around the community as someone who caused marriage problems; apparently, she drew husbands away. She came up to me after church a few times to ask spiritual questions, and she seemed legitimate in wanting to grow in her relationship with God. But one of Paula's friends was concerned and told Paula she needed to watch the woman, because she might try to make a play for me. Paula's friend began to tell her about the lady's reputation, and Paula listened to the gossip. Not too long after that in a Wednesday night service, Paula was sitting adjacent to this woman with the reputation, and the Lord began to convict her about participating in gossip. He told Paula to go to the woman and repent for gossiping about her. Paula was shocked, and for the whole service, she wrestled with what she believed the Lord was asking her to do. After the service ended, she gave in, went up to the woman, and repented for participating in gossip against her. The woman started to cry. "During the service," she said, "I asked the Lord for someone who could help me, someone I could trust." She looked at Paula. "I now know I can trust you because of your heart to confess your sin." And Paula realized the importance of being obedient to the Lord even if what God is saying sounds absurd.

Obedience is not learned in good times but in tough times. It is founded in our hearts when we feel exposed in the wilderness. Even Jesus' obedience was established in the fire of suffering:

> "In the days of His flesh, He offered up both prayers and supplications with loud crying and tears to the One able to save Him from death, and He was heard because of His piety. Although He was a Son, He learned obedience from the things which He suffered."   — Hebrews 5:7–8

Remember that God wants to bring us into the promised land. He delights in the prosperity of His people.[12] As a good Father, He loves richly supplying His kids with all good things to enjoy.[13] Yet before He can bring us fully into the promise, the character of obedience has to be founded deeply within us, so we do not destroy the promised land or be destroyed by the promised land.

One of the benefits of obedience is victorious spiritual warfare. Whenever our obedience is "complete," we are able to punish the disobedience of the spiritual realm.[14] This means we can remove the spiritual strongholds the enemy would potentially use to hinder us.

The man or woman who has a heart of obedience can be trusted with all kinds of resources. A friend in real estate development shared with me an experience that taught him about the importance of being obedient and honest in all matters, both small and great. One day he was having lunch with a large property developer and an owner of a large construction company. The developer was looking for someone to do construction work for him. They talked over the meal, and everything seemed to be going well in the negotiations. As they finished the main course, they decided to get pieces of pie for dessert. Afterward, the contractor picked up the ticket, which the waitress had delivered before the pie. She had forgotten to give them a new ticket that included the pie, and the contractor said, "It's only a piece of pie. Not a big deal." And he proceeded to pay for the meal without telling the cashier about the dessert.

After the contractor left, my friend looked at the developer and said, "You aren't going to hire him to do your work, are you?"

The developer said, "No. If a person cannot be trusted with a piece of pie, he cannot be trusted with millions of dollars in business."

God is with us in the wilderness. His provisions come from His presence. Whether or not we understand what is going on, obedience to God and His Word is an absolute. In everything we do, we want to move in the direction of knowing God and His character, for these form our foundation for obedience:

"Trust in the Lord with all your heart
And do not lean on your own understanding.
In all your ways acknowledge Him,
And He will make your paths straight."
— Proverbs 3:5–6

Developing a Mindset of Blessing and Wealth

Another purpose of the wilderness is to equip us with the power to make wealth. This often means that God needs to revamp our current mindsets.

> *"Otherwise, you may say in your heart, 'My power and the strength of my hand made me this wealth.' But you shall remember the Lord your God, for it is He who is giving you power to make wealth, that He may confirm His covenant which He swore to your fathers, as it is this day."*
> — Deuteronomy 8:17–18

The "power to make wealth" is a pretty phenomenal statement. It is not that our Father simply gives us wealth—it is that He gives us the power to make wealth. When Israel stepped into the Promised Land, God changed His methods of providing for them. He no longer "spoon-fed" them with manna and quail. Instead, they had to generate wealth and provision with the resources He set up for them.

I have a friend who works for an international relief organization that helps feed the poor and needy all over the world. He told me poverty at its foundational level is not a lack of resources but a mindset. Wars and disasters cause hunger, but those things can be overcome with help. Poverty, meanwhile, is a way of thinking that must be overcome with a revelation of truth, which is why his organization devotes so much of its resources to schools and the support of churches.

The subject of blessing and wealth can be tricky because the human heart is easily swayed by greed and the love of money. Remember that the greatest test we could ever face is success. It can come in many forms: jobs, finances, relationships, ministries, and the highest blessing of all—the opportunity to participate in God's eternal Kingdom. The key to utilizing the power to make wealth is dependency on the Lord, and it is in the wilderness such dependency is developed and released in our lives.

Whenever we talk about the power to make wealth, two simple but foundational questions arise: What is wealth, and what is the power to make it? If we are going to change our mindsets about wealth, we need to understand what it is and how it works.

Wealth in Relationships

The Word of God often talks about "wealth" in the form of relationships. The greatest wealth a person could have is family and friends, and we should think of our relationships as resources.

One of my all-time favorite movies is *It's a Wonderful Life*. James Stewart plays a man named George Bailey who has wanted to be rich and successful since childhood. But every time he has an opportunity to be successful, he sacrifices his desires to help other people. The movie climaxes when George is faced with a dramatic financial crisis, which pushes him to the brink of suicide. But George finds out that the greatest wealth a person could have is family and friends. In the very last scene of the movie, George's family, friends, and business associates are gathered around him, and George's brother proposes a toast: "A toast to my big brother, George, the richest man in town!"

As George discovered, the greatest thing we can possess is relationships. What made George successful was that he gave of himself all throughout the movie. Unknowingly, he was making an investment in the accumulation of true wealth. Being rich means loving and sharing with others. It is not the number of or the type of relationships we have; it is what we do with those relationships that is important. Paul wrote that we should pursue what is "life indeed":

> *"Instruct those who are rich in this present world not to be conceited or to fix their hope on the uncertainty of riches, but on God, who richly supplies us with all things to enjoy. Instruct them to do good, to be rich in good works, to be generous and ready to share, storing up for themselves the treasure of a good foundation for the future, so that they may take hold of that which is life indeed."*
>
> — 1 Timothy 6:17–19

But again, it isn't the amount of wealth we give away that makes us rich; it is the heart behind the giving. Jesus pointed out a widow who put everything she had into the temple treasury. The rich were giving substantial gifts, but she gave out of her poverty. He told the disciples, *"This poor widow put in more than all of them; for they all out of their surplus put into the offering; but she out of her poverty put in all that she had to live on"* (Luke 21:3–4). In other words, she was accumulating true wealth.

God assigns to each of us people who take on important roles in our lives, and these people are a source of wealth. A godly wife is a reward[15] and more valuable than jewels.[16] But the reward isn't so much that a man has a wife; the wealth is found in the person, not the role. I cannot describe how valuable Paula has been to me. She is a treasure to my heart, and I wouldn't accomplish nearly as much in my life if not for her.

One of the joys of being a dad is watching your children grow up and walk in what you prayed and trained them for. When Paula and I visit our son, daughter-in-law, and their kids, my heart rejoices at what I see. I am amazed at how my son, Shea, loves and serves his wife, Lile. As I do my grandfatherly duty and play with the kids on the floor or chase them around the house, Shea and Lile often sit on the couch talking and laughing together. I watch Shea serve his wife by allowing her to sleep late in the mornings when he doesn't have to work. He gets up with the kids and cooks breakfast for them. He faithfully plays with and takes care of them, empowering them with the understanding that their dad really loves them. He works at his regular job, only to come home and do side work to make extra money for his family after the kids and Lile are in bed.

As I watch him do these things, I wonder, Where did he learn to walk like this with his family? I feel like he exceeds anything I ever walked in as a dad and husband. I think back through the years when Paula and I were raising him, and I remember the hard times he faced and the wildernesses that helped shape him. On many occasions, I wished I could have made things easier for him. There were moments as his dad when I cried and prayed before the Lord in secret for my son. But standing on this side of fatherhood and looking at the growth of my children, I can say with assurance that God never gives up, and He fills our every gap as parents with His grace and mercy.

However it comes, the blessing of God is a form of wealth, and children are a tremendous blessing.[17] Parents, brothers, sisters, friends, and spiritual family are an amazing source of wealth in our lives:

> *"Oil and perfume make the heart glad,*
> *So a man's counsel is sweet to his friend.*
> *Do not forsake your own friend or your father's friend,*
> *And do not go to your brother's house in the day of your*
> *calamity; Better is a neighbor who is near*
> *than a brother far away."* — Proverbs 27:9–10

When I think about the people I know and love, I feel like George Bailey, the richest man in the world.

Wealth in Physical Resources

Wealth can also be money, houses, securities, land, and so forth. Physical resources obviously are an important part of our everyday lives, yet the most important thing in life has nothing to do with acquiring physical riches.[13] We use physical resources as a means to support and maintain true wealth, which is where a wilderness comes in. In the wilderness, we learn what true wealth is and how to use it.

Wealth in Spiritual and Soulish Resources

The last type of wealth is something we can't actually "make," such as money. We can simply steward these things: the wealth of time,[18] the wealth of faith.[19] the wealth of the Holy Spirit's gifts,[20] the wealth of the physical body,[21] and the wealth of words.[22] It is important to think of these things as wealth, because they are some of the most important gifts God gives us. Any time we enter a wilderness, we will have to consider the stewardship of this type of wealth.

What Is the Power to Make Wealth?

The power to make wealth can be broken down into two facets: the ordering of wealth and the investing or generating of wealth. We could fill volumes with information about these two topics, so what I've written here is just a brief overview.

Ordering of Wealth

When we order wealth, we use our God-given authority to direct the flow of our resources:

> *"He who offers a sacrifice of thanksgiving honors Me;*
> *And to him who orders his way aright*
> *I shall show the salvation of God."*   — Psalm 50:23

> *"So teach us to number our days,*
> *That we may present to You a heart of wisdom."*
> — Psalm 90:12

We order wealth by determining the priority and value of the resources God has given us. After determining the priority and value, we then use our authority to choose what will flow into our lives and how we will invest these resources. A budget is a practical application of the ordering of wealth. Planning our time with the use of a schedule also falls into this category.

Generating Wealth

The other facet of the power to make wealth involves the blessing of the Lord, which causes resources to flow into our lives:

> *"How blessed is the man who does not walk*
> *in the counsel of the wicked,*
> *Nor stand in the path of sinners,*
> *Nor sit in the seat of scoffers!*
> *But his delight is in the law of the Lord,*
> *And in His law he meditates day and night.*

He will be like a tree firmly planted by streams of water,
Which yields its fruit in its season
And its leaf does not wither;
And in whatever he does, he prospers."

— Psalm 1:1–3

Our heavenly Father longs to see us, His children, blessed in the vocations we have chosen. He wants us to prosper in everything we put our hands and minds to.

"Let them shout for joy and rejoice,
who favor my vindication;
And let them say continually,
'The Lord be magnified,
Who delights in the prosperity of His servant.'"

— Psalm 35:27

"They drink their fill of the abundance of Your house;
And You give them to drink of the river of Your delights."

— Psalm 36:8

When our Father blesses the work of our hands, He is glorified, and the world sees His goodness.

As I stated earlier, there are many excellent books, audio teachings, and other resources that address the ordering and generating of wealth. The important matter to remember is that a wilderness is a pathway the Lord uses to prepare us for the future. Our Father loves us dearly, and in the midst of a sinful, broken world, He gets us ready for the promised land.

Notes / Reference Scriptures

A. This may sound like a broad topic, but it boils down to having your needs met in Jesus. You can learn more about needs in my book entitled - *Jesus: The Filler of Needs*. For more information, visit dealingjesus.org.

1. Deuteronomy 8:5
2. Jeremiah 29:11
3. Deuteronomy 8:7-10
4. 1 Samuel 17:39
5. Proverbs 17:3
6. Deuteronomy 8:3
7. 2 Corinthians 10:3-5; Ephesians 6:12
8. 1 Thessalonians 2:4
9. 1 Corinthians 4:1
10. Genesis 11:30
11. Genesis 12:10
12. Psalm 35:27
13. 1 Timothy 6:17
14. 2 Corinthians 10:6
15. Ecclesiastes 9:9
16. Proverbs 31:10-11
17. Psalm 127:4-5
18. Psalm 90:14
19. Romans 12:3
20. 1 Peter 4:10-11
21. 1 Corinthians 6:19-20
22. Matthew 12:36-37

PART TWO

The Wilderness Season

A Closer Look at the Different Wildernesses Found in Scripture

"Therefore, behold, I will allure her,
Bring her into the wilderness
And speak kindly to her." — Hosea 2:14

We should think about the wilderness experience in this way: If the Lord is good, and He gives only good gifts, and He is somehow involved with the wilderness—then the wilderness has to be something good. Every characteristic of God's heart has at its root the pulse of a loving heavenly Father who wants to see His children find life.

In this section, we are going to look at the four different types of wildernesses found in Scripture and how God is moving in each one. He is the God of redemption, which means that He is working to cause all situations and circumstances to turn out for our good.

5 The Wilderness of Transition

Paula and I have a friend named Carla who was a part of our church family, Dwelling Place Fellowship, back in its early days. She experienced dramatic transformation; God healed her of wounds and lies she believed, and she received several words about her ministry and destiny.

Eventually God directed her and her family to a different part of the country. They moved several hundred miles away from Blacksburg, and all at once, Carla found herself in the middle of a wilderness of transition. In our community, she had many relationships and close friends, but in the new location, she couldn't seem to develop relationships like she had had before. She didn't have the Internet for a few months and initially didn't have a cell phone either. Two of her children started school right away, and with her husband at work all day at his new job, she felt very alone.

Carla and her husband tried a few business ventures, but they didn't pan out. Her husband's new job wasn't what he thought it would be, and he began to realize it wasn't what he wanted to do. All of this created a sense of uncertainty in Carla, and she was very humbled during this time. Out of necessity, she began to rely more on the Lord. She felt compelled to, because all her other support systems had been removed. The Lord was able to speak to her, correct her, teach her, and comfort her. She began to tell others about the healing she had received and what she had learned in Blacksburg. Slowly, she started to walk in the ministry and destiny God had proclaimed to her. She no longer needed friendships in an unhealthy way but could enjoy them in right alignment.

Out of nowhere, God provided her husband with the job of a lifetime in Arizona. Things moved quickly, and Carla and her family were plucked out of the wilderness and put into an oasis in the real desert — and they loved it. They quickly found a little church plant that was a perfect fit for them, and they became a crucial relational foundation in this new church where they presently serve as leaders. The wilderness they encountered set them up for the fullness God had for them, and they were able to walk in their destiny in the Promised Land.

The wilderness of transition is a season in which the Lord's blessing, gifting, ministry, and destiny are birthed, established, and released in our lives. God led Carla into this wilderness so He could form within her the reality and character of His Word.

When Israel came out of Egypt, they had a slave mentality[1] and thought within the context of unbelief,[2] disobedience,[3] and defeat.[4] After God radically freed them from slavery, they hoped to enter the Promised Land — but that simply wasn't possible. Walking in unbelief, disobedience, defeat, and slavery, how could they handle the good things God promised them? Before they could enter the land, the Lord first had to lead them through a season of transition.[5] He was preparing them for their future, so they would be able to shake off the mantle of slavery and walk in faith, obedience, victory, and authority.

The Lord's heart is to bless us. He wants to be extravagant with us, but He is a good Father, not a reckless one, so it is important to Him that we be prepared to receive His blessings. In the wilderness of transition, we learn that it is the Lord alone who fulfills our needs. When we know He is our Source, we will be obedient to Him in any situation, particularly in the promised land.

We go through a wilderness of transition when it is time for one season to end and another to begin.

Examples of the Wilderness of Transitions

Let's look at three examples of the wilderness of transition found in Scripture.

Abraham and the Promised Land

The Lord promised Abraham that his descendants would become a great nation and he would receive a land of promise.[6] Abraham believed Him, but when he responded to the Lord's word and left his homeland to step into his promise, he discovered the land was inhabited by the Canaanites and was in the middle of a severe famine.[7] Also, despite the promise he had from God about his descendants, Abraham's wife was barren.

All three of these obstacles were different forms of the wilderness of transition. And it was in these wildernesses that Abraham became the father of our faith.

Peter and His Destiny

Jesus affirmed Peter's future ministry in Matthew 16 in a dramatic way—and immediately, Peter was dropped into a wilderness of transition. Following Peter's confession about Jesus, Jesus rebuked him, calling him Satan (or adversary). Later on, Peter denied Jesus three times, and after the crucifixion, Peter just retreated. He went back to what he had known before, which was fishing.[8]

When Jesus appeared on the seashore, He healed Peter's heart of the denial and commissioned him to the ministry of caring for His people. Peter had denied Jesus three times around a charcoal fire, and three times around a charcoal fire Jesus declared Peter's ministry into existence. Emotions and the sense of smell are two of the strongest imprinters of information on our hearts. We can easily remember events that accompany powerful emotions or strong smells. Every time Peter smelled a charcoal fire, it likely reminded him of that dreadful night of his denial — until Jesus redeemed it for him. Jesus declared forgiveness into Peter and healed his heart of feelings of failure.

This season of transition was crucial for Peter. Before the wilderness, Peter was a self-confident, self-sufficient man, but after the wilderness, Peter became a man of God dependent upon the name of Jesus and the power of the Holy Spirit.[9]

Jesus After His Baptism

After His baptism, Jesus entered a wilderness of transition that lasted forty days, during which the foundation and character of His ministry were established. He didn't have any sin to work out of His life; instead, He rested in the reality and power of His Father's Word, and that Word sustained Him.

Purposes of the Wilderness of Transition

A wilderness of transition has three major purposes:

1. It tests the word we received from God (it empowers the word to become ours).
2. It establishes the character necessary to sustain the word.
3. It gives us hearts of humility, through which we realize God alone is our Provider.

We won't find all three purposes in every wilderness of transition, but at least one of them will be evident in any given case. Let's look at each of them more closely.

Testing the Word

When God speaks to us, His word will be tested, for every word of God is tested.[10] When we first hear a word from God, it sits in our conscious minds but isn't established in the depths of our hearts. It isn't ours yet. The process of testing the word is how we take ownership of what God has spoken to us. The word will be tested in the wilderness. In the parable of the sower, the second type of soil represents people who hear God's word and experience hardship because of it:

> *"The one on whom seed was sown on the rocky places, this is the man who hears the word and immediately receives it with joy; yet he has no firm root in himself, but is only temporary, and when affliction or persecution arises because of the word, immediately he falls away."*
> — Matthew 13:20–21

The testing of a word produces a wilderness of transition. When God the Father spoke words of glory and honor over His Son, the Holy Spirit immediately led Jesus into a wilderness "to be tempted by the devil."[11] Hebrews 5:8 says, *"Although He was a Son, He learned obedience from the things which He suffered."* Personally, I think the writer of Hebrews at least in part was referencing Jesus' time in the wilderness, when the devil tempted Him. Luke wrote that Jesus went into the wilderness full of the Holy Spirit,[12] and He came out of the wilderness walking in the power of the Holy Spirit.[13] What was the difference? His Father's word had been established within Him.

After God revealed his destiny as a ruler, Joseph entered an extended season of wilderness thanks to his brothers, who sold him as a slave. He was later thrown in prison for a crime he didn't commit—why? *"They afflicted his feet with fetters, he himself was laid in irons; until the time that his word came to pass, the word of the Lord tested him"* (Psalm 105:18–19). He was tested by the word of the Lord.

Abraham had a word from God about his future son at a time when his wife was barren, but he allowed the word to take root within him and did not lose his faith. He *"believed God, and it was credited to him as righteousness"* (Romans 4:3). When God speaks a rhema word (that is, when He speaks directly to a person), a time of wilderness could occur because the wilderness is what establishes the truth of that word in our hearts.

The Character of the Word

A word of God is tested so His character can be founded within us. When God told Abraham that he was going to be the father of many nations, Abraham's character was far from the reality of that word. He lied twice regarding Sarah, his wife. He tried to negotiate with God so his nephew could be his heir. He also grew impatient and gave way to his wife's pressuring, having a son with her maid. But God worked with Abraham to grow him into the man he was called to be.[14]

If we know Jesus Christ as our Lord and Savior, we are destined to be conformed into His image.[15] Along with this destiny to look like Jesus, we are given a ministry to make disciples.[16] That ministry is a ministry of love that involves imparting our lives to others.[17] The Life that works within us is the Life we impart. God instills within us His DNA through His Word. What God wants to entrust to us demands a lot of responsibility and character. Before He can entrust us with His blessings and His children, we need to be able to carry the weight of that responsibility. Paul wrote that we are "servants of Christ and stewards of the mysteries of God" and it is "required" of stewards that they be found trustworthy.[18] He also wrote that these people should *first be tested; then let them serve as deacons if they are beyond reproach"* (1 Timothy 3:10). The character in our hearts determines who we are and what we will do.

How is His character established within us? First, we need to know the content of our hearts. Do we believe anything that doesn't line up with the word God has spoken over us? Thinking and believing what God says about us is different than knowing and experiencing it. In a wilderness of transition, when all our human props and sources have been removed, the programming of our hearts is revealed.[19] True change cannot occur until we know what needs to be changed. If a person has cancer, the doctors need to discover the cancer's origin so they can administer a treatment. Similarly, God gave the Law of Moses to reveal sin so the sin could be dealt with. When the content of our hearts is revealed, we can partner with the Lord to change what needs changing.[A]

Second, remember that God causes all things to turn out for our good. He uses the trials and temptations we encounter to establish His character in our hearts.

The Greek words *peirazo* (verb) and *peirasmos* (noun) have the same root and therefore the same meaning. They can be translated as "temptation" and "trial," which have different meanings in the English language, but in Greek they literally mean "to puncture" or "to pass through." A person standing in front of a doorway is being offered an opportunity to pass through the door. That is what it means to be tempted. We have a door in front of us, and we can choose to go through it or not.

James wrote that God does not tempt us with evil: *"Let no one say when he is tempted, 'I am being tempted by God'; for God cannot be tempted by evil, and He Himself does not tempt anyone"* (James 1:13). God will not put before us an opportunity to sin; however, the devil will. If we turn to God instead of the sin, He will change the situation and use it to form His character within us.

One day while I was praying, the Lord communicated to me that He was imparting into me the image, or character, of His Son. I saw a big block of wax I knew was my heart. It didn't have any form or shape to it. Then I saw a coin being pressed against the wax, and I thought of the time when the Pharisees questioned Jesus about paying taxes. He asked them for a coin and said, "Whose image is on this?" A coin carries the image of a person being honored. God's Word is like a coin in that it bears a particular facet of Jesus' image. As He "presses" His Word into us, we begin to replicate that image.

Next I saw the devil take a hot wood-burning stylist and press it against the coin. An uncomfortable amount of heat began to fill the metal, and I sensed I had a choice to make. I could decide the coin was too painful, that it was too hot to handle, and pull it away from my heart before the image of Jesus was complete. Or I could keep my hold on God's Word, even though it would be uncomfortable and potentially difficult for me. After a few minutes, the devil gave up, and the hot stylist was removed. When the coin was brought away, the wax bore its image. That is essentially what happens in a wilderness. God spoke to us, the word is tested, and it is during the test that the image of Jesus is impressed into the fabric of our beings.

The Holy Spirit led Jesus into the wilderness to be tempted by the devil.[20] If we gave this only a surface glance, we might think God was teaming up with Satan, but He was actually setting Jesus up to be invulnerable to the devil's schemes. If Jesus could resist the devil's temptations before He began His ministry — before He was carrying the spiritual weight brought by ministry — He would be able to stand even with the weight of the world's sin upon Him. When God takes us into a wilderness and allows Satan to try to steal His word from our hearts,[21] it produces within us the resilience to stand as strong men and women of God.

A vaccine exposes our bodies to a weak form of the disease in order to build our immunity to the disease. When our loving Father allows the devil to tempt us, He is giving us an opportunity to become immune to that particular area of sin. We know He won't allow us to be tempted beyond what we can handle. In every temptation, He will give us a "way of escape also."[22] As His word to us is tested, proven character is established in our hearts,[23] and we become perfect and complete, lacking in nothing.[24] That is the outcome of temptation and victory.

God cannot, nor will He ever, tempt us to sin, but He will give us the opportunity to believe Him. He did this with Abraham when He asked him to offer his promised son, Isaac, as a sacrifice.[25] He was giving Abraham the chance to believe Him and be established as a man of faith.[26]

In a wilderness of transition, the Lord offered Israel the opportunity to establish their character as a people who were obedient and faithful to Him. They had the opportunity to be a people whose love and faith were not dictated by their circumstances:

> *"Then he cried out to the Lord, and the Lord showed him a tree; and he threw it into the waters, and the waters became sweet. There He made for them a statute and regulation, and there He tested them."*   — Exodus 15:25

> *"Then the Lord said to Moses, 'Behold, I will rain bread from heaven for you; and the people shall go out and gather a day's portion every day, that I may test them, whether or not they will walk in My instruction.'"*   — Exodus 16:4

In a wilderness, the Lord sometimes will allow the enemy to tempt us to sin, but He always regulates the degree of the temptation. The temptation can either be the doorway to sin or the doorway to faith. It is up to us. The doorway to faith is our opportunity to become perfect and complete.

A Humble Heart

When God takes us into a wilderness of transition, He is offering us a great gift—a heart of humility. Two basic things comprise a humble heart: dependency and perspective. A humble heart is totally dependent on God and the Body of Christ, and it sees itself in proper perspective, recognizing its need for relationship with other people. In the wilderness of transition, God works in us to develop our character, so we are completely dependent upon Him to fulfill and supply our needs:

> *"In the wilderness He fed you manna which your fathers did not know, that He might humble you and that He might test you, to do good for you in the end. Otherwise, you may say in your heart, 'My power and the strength of my hand made me this wealth.' But you shall remember the Lord your God, for it is He who is giving you power to make wealth, that He may confirm His covenant which He swore to your fathers, as it is this day."*   — Deuteronomy 8:16–18

We cannot enter the promised land self-dependent and self-confident. Two of the greatest temptations we face in life are success and prosperity. If we start to believe that our success is our own doing, it opens a doorway for pride, which causes us to lose our dependency on the Lord. We forget that He is our Father and Provider, the One who supplies all our needs.[27]

In the wilderness of transition, we can fully establish our faith and dependency in the Lord to meet our needs. Jesus rebuked the church at Laodicea for being lukewarm in their faith, a situation that arose because they were comfortable in life and thought they did not have any needs:

> *"'I know your deeds, that you are neither cold nor hot; I wish that you were cold or hot. So because you are lukewarm, and neither hot nor cold, I will spit you out of My mouth. Because you say, "I am rich, and have become wealthy, and have need of nothing," and you do not know that you are wretched and miserable and poor and blind and naked, I advise you to buy from Me gold refined by fire so that you may become rich, and white garments so that you may clothe yourself, and that the shame of your nakedness will not be revealed; and eye salve to anoint your eyes so that you may see.'"* — Revelation 3:15–18

They had become rich in the world's goods, and it had sedated them. Their wealth kept them from longing for the true riches found in God. Our trust in God needs to be constant. When we experience His love in the wilderness, our belief and trust in Him become real; they are no longer something we have only heard of or read about. We have experienced the reality of God's provision and care in the midst of uncertainty, and we believe and trust Him, because we know Him. Jesus must always be our Source of fulfillment, not our circumstances.

After God spoke to Joseph about being a ruler, every step of Joseph's wilderness related to being ruled and out of control. He was ruled by his brothers and had no say when they threw him in the pit and later sold him. He was a servant in the house of Potiphar and was helpless when accused of something he didn't do. He was ruled in the prison, and the men he ministered to didn't even remember him. At the end of his time in the wilderness, he had deep humility and dependency on God:

> *"Pharaoh said to Joseph, 'I have had a dream, but no one can interpret it; and I have heard it said about you, that when you hear a dream you can interpret it.' Joseph then answered Pharaoh, saying, 'It is not in me; God will give Pharaoh a favorable answer.'"* — Genesis 41:15–16

Joseph had matured. He didn't seek to be recognized. He sought only to glorify God.

Paul faced different types of wildernesses in his life, and as a result, he, too, had a humble heart. He knew who his Supplier was: *"My God will supply all your needs according to His riches in glory in Christ Jesus"* (Philippians 4:19). When humility is established, exaltation will follow.[28] God's heart is to see us exalted into the purposes and plans He has for us. True humility doesn't look like shrinking back or losing hope for change — not at all. Humility is strength. When we are willing to be humble, we are stepping under God's mighty hand, so He can exalt us.

Results of a Wilderness of Transition

What is the outcome of the wilderness of transition? We are prepared to enter a new phase of life.

We Are Empowered

The wilderness of transition empowers us to fulfill the destiny we are about to enter. An example of this is the wilderness Jesus experienced after John baptized Him. Luke's account shows four different ways the Holy Spirit ministered to Jesus during this time:

1. The Holy Spirit came upon Jesus, which related to His commissioning:

> *"The Holy Spirit **descended upon Him** in bodily form like a dove, and a voice came out of heaven, 'You are My beloved Son, in You I am well-pleased.'"*
> — Luke 3:22 (emphasis added)

2. Jesus was "full of the Holy Spirit."[12] He had been on the mountaintop with God, saturated in His Father's presence. Often before we enter a wilderness of transition, we have a mountaintop experience with the Lord.

3. The Holy Spirit led Jesus in the wilderness.[12] This statement reaffirms the reality that a wilderness is not a place of abandonment; God's presence continually guides us. The verb tense in Luke 4:1 communicates that the Holy Spirit was continually leading Jesus; it was a time when Jesus was completely dependent on the Holy Spirit to guide Him and get Him through. Humility is a heart of total dependency on God.

4. Luke 4:14 reveals a new dynamic between Jesus and the Holy Spirit—Jesus returned to Galilee in the Spirit's power. The result of Jesus humbling Himself and accepting the Holy Spirit's leadership was the power of the Spirit being manifested in His life. Jesus could have developed a self-sufficient attitude and declared, "I'm God. I can do this. I can make it." But even though He was a Son, He humbled Himself to another's leadership. When we humble ourselves under God's hand, He will empower us to fulfill the things He has called us to accomplish.

Are You in a Wilderness of Transition?

When we realize we are entering a wilderness, we often think, What have I done wrong? But a wilderness of transition isn't punishment; it is an act of love. The Holy Spirit carried Jesus into the wilderness so His ministry on the earth could begin.[12] When Joseph was unjustly thrown in prison, it was not because he had done something wrong—it was the huge destiny before him that put him in that wilderness.

God's heart is that we understand His ways.[29] For Jesus and Joseph, the wilderness was God's way to position them for the greatness He had prepared for them. When we understand God's ways, we understand that He is good and He is working to cause everything in our lives to turn out for our benefit. God's way and God's will are to make us great:

> *"Both riches and honor come from You, and You rule over all, and in Your hand is power and might; and it lies in Your hand to make great and to strengthen everyone."*
> — 1 Chronicles 29:12

As we come to understand that God's work within us is not meant to hurt us, we can set our faith to partner with Him, eagerly embracing everything He wants to do in us.[30] The wilderness of transition is our Father's heart to position us for destiny.

How do we know when we are in a wilderness? Here are a few clues.

You Heard God's Voice

Has God spoken to you about your future?

That is one of the main ways we can know we are in a wilderness of transition. Every word God speaks to us will be tested in some way, and that test usually involves this specific wilderness.[10] The wilderness we experience will somehow relate to the revelation we received. After God called Jesus His beloved Son, Jesus faced a wilderness and temptations that were in relationship to that word. After God spoke to him about his future, Abraham entered a wilderness. After Jesus affirmed Peter, Peter found himself in a wilderness. All of these men had one thing in common: They had words from the Lord regarding the future.

In the spring of 1985, God put it on my heart to go into ministry full time, and I went through a series of wildernesses to prepare me for what was coming. One wilderness came as a result of Paula's doubt that I was called into full-time ministry. She even told the ladies in her prayer group to pray for me because I had it in my head to go into ministry full time. Later, after God showed her that yes, we were supposed to head that direction, we faced a financial wilderness. The next wilderness involved the seminary I wanted to attend, which was strong in biblical exegesis and languages. They refused to accept me because of my beliefs regarding the present-day working of the Holy Spirit's gifts.

It was a difficult time, yet everything that happened was in relationship to the word God had given me. God spoke to me clearly and solidified His call in my life. Many times since,

I have returned to those words and the affirmations the Lord gave me during that season. In the winter of 1986, my family and I finally moved to Texas to begin seminary.

If God gives us a word about wealth, it is possible we could encounter a time of financial drought, because He is establishing His character in our hearts concerning that word. If He gives us a word about relationships, it is probable that we will go through a wilderness regarding relationships. If He gives us a word about a future in ministry, most likely our ministry opportunities will dry up for a season. The number-one indicator of a wilderness of transition is a word or dream from the Lord.

God Warns You in Advance

When Jesus entered the wilderness, the Holy Spirit was the One who led Him there. Jesus knew what was going on because the Holy Spirit told Him where to go.

Sometimes God will tell us about an upcoming wilderness of transition. He lets us know we are in a season of change. The wilderness of transition comes about, and not too long afterward, we move into something new.

You Start Something New

As we talked about, when God speaks to us concerning who we are or what He is doing in our lives, a wilderness often occurs in relation to the revelation. At times, however, we begin a ministry, start a business, or otherwise take a step forward in destiny, and then the wilderness starts. The wilderness for Abraham occurred as he stepped into the promise, not before. The Lord told him to leave his homeland and go to the Promised Land, but when Abraham arrived, the land was experiencing a famine.[31] Things became difficult.

Sometimes as we begin to walk in our dreams, it can seem like they are just one big wilderness. We don't know what we're doing, or what is happening, or how to make things work. The uncertainties can cause us to question whether or not we made the right decision to pursue what God put on our hearts.

But we shouldn't give up. The wilderness of transition is God's way of preparing us to fulfill our dreams. When we have taken a significant step in our lives—we moved, we entered the ministry, we began to walk in a specific gifting or blessing—and suddenly, we begin to experience the characteristics of a wilderness, it is a good indication that it is a wilderness of transition. The hardships we walk through will help us reach our end goals, whatever those are for each of us.

Responding in the Wilderness of Transition

Once we realize we're in a wilderness of transition, we know what to do.

Our response in the wilderness determines whether or not we walk out God's plans and heart for our lives. Israel's response in the wilderness did not propel them into the Promised Land but into a second wilderness: the wilderness of sin and death. Jesus, on the other hand, held to His Father's word and embraced righteousness and truth. He came out of the wilderness in the Holy Spirit's power.

The following scriptural principles are keys to success in any season of life, but they are particularly relevant for a wilderness of transition.

Joy and Thanksgiving

> *"Because Your lovingkindness is better than life,*
> *My lips will praise You.*
> *So I will bless You as long as I live;*
> *I will lift up my hands in Your name.*
> *My soul is satisfied as with marrow and fatness,*
> *And my mouth offers praises with joyful lips."*
> — Psalm 63:3–5

David is one of my favorite examples of someone giving praise in the wilderness. When he was in a wilderness of transition—it happened to be a literal wilderness in Judah—his response to the situation was to praise and give thanks to the Lord. Praise and thanksgiving set our hearts and minds on God and refocus us, so we are able to take refuge in Him.

> *"Rejoice always; pray without ceasing; in everything give thanks; for this is God's will for you in Christ Jesus."*
> — 1 Thessalonians 5:16–18

Whatever the reason for the wilderness, we need to face it with an attitude of joy and thanksgiving, for living in joy and thanksgiving is God's will for our lives. When Paul, James, and Peter wrote about trials and tribulations, all three first mentioned the principle of rejoicing. Joy and thanksgiving aren't the usual feelings that arise in our hearts when we think of the wilderness, but James wrote that we can be joyful even at the thought of a trial:

> *"Consider it all joy, my brethren, when you encounter various trials, knowing that the testing of your faith produces endurance. And let endurance have its perfect result, so that you may be perfect and complete, lacking in nothing."*
> — James 1:2–4

Trials and temptations often occur in a wilderness of transition. The key that releases joy in our hearts is realizing what God wants us to understand—we need the revelation He wants to give us concerning what is happening and what is about to happen. We also need to know that we aren't being punished or abandoned. Instead, we are about to pass through a doorway for our perfection. We can "greatly rejoice" when we are in a trial or wilderness because it is an opportunity for our faith to be purified and established in Jesus' glory and honor:

> *"In this you greatly rejoice, even though now for a little while, if necessary, you have been distressed by various trials, so that the proof of your faith, being more precious than*

gold which is perishable, even though tested by fire, may be found to result in praise and glory and honor at the revelation of Jesus Christ."   — 1 Peter 1:6–7

We can think about it like this. A football player can look forward to lifting weights because he knows the "pain" he endures now gives him the opportunity to succeed with what he loves: playing football. No wilderness or trial is a random event. All of them are specific opportunities for us to be established in faith, now and for eternity.

An attitude of joy and thanksgiving is powerful in our lives. First, it keeps our minds set on the Lord's presence and provisions, not on our circumstances. When David was in the wilderness, he continually faced threats on his life and lacked the resources to care for himself and those associated with him, but he trusted in the unfailing character of God.[32] He believed God's word to him, and that word eventually came to pass. He rejoiced as he recalled God's presence and the way He had provided for him in the past.

When we choose to rejoice, we release into our lives the joy of the Lord, which is our strength.[33] An attitude of joy and thanksgiving keeps us from the doorway to destruction, which is built by grumbling and complaining. We can see evidence of this door in the lives of the children of Israel during their wilderness of transition:

> *"Now the people became like those who complain of adversity in the hearing of the Lord; and when the Lord heard it, His anger was kindled, and the fire of the Lord burned among them and consumed some of the outskirts of the camp."*   — Numbers 11:1

> *"Nor let us try the Lord, as some of them did, and were destroyed by the serpents. Nor grumble, as some of them did, and were destroyed by the destroyer."*
>   — 1 Corinthians 10:9–10

Victory in the wilderness of transition is built on an attitude of thanksgiving and joy!

Contentment

God will provide in the wilderness. We never have a reason to worry or fear concerning His provision, but if we're not careful, the uncertainty of the wilderness can cause us to begin to resent His provision, as the children of Israel experienced. They began to grumble about the manna and quail the Lord miraculously provided for them, and as their resentment grew, they lost their contentment:

> *"The rabble who were among them had greedy desires; and also the sons of Israel wept again and said, 'Who will give us meat to eat? We remember the fish which we used to eat free in Egypt, the cucumbers and the melons and the leeks and the onions and the garlic, but now our appetite is gone. There is nothing at all to look at except this manna.'"*
>
> — Numbers 11:4–6

It is dangerous for us to lose contentment, because such a loss can cause us to long for the things of the past in an unhealthy way. In our hearts, we want to turn back to what we knew before and let go of our faith that God's best waits for us just down the road.[34]

The apostle Paul knew times of ease and times of intense difficulty, and he learned the secret for surviving both with his heart intact:

> *"Not that I speak from want, for I have learned to be content in whatever circumstances I am. I know how to get along with humble means, and I also know how to live in prosperity; in any and every circumstance I have learned the secret of being filled and going hungry, both of having abundance and suffering need."*   — Philippians 4:11–12

Contentment is not something we generate. Contentment is a result that comes from having our needs met. If I go to a steak house and have prime rib with sautéed mushrooms and a baked potato smothered with sour cream and chives, and then I follow it up with one of my favorite desserts, I will be content physically. I will not have the desire for anything more.

That is what God does for our souls. True contentment comes from being saturated with the fullness and sufficiency of Jesus Christ. He loves us with an everlasting love.[35] He is not going to abandon us.[36] He promised He would direct our steps.[37] He is always faithful to us.[38] He has given everything to see us walk in the fullness of glory.[39] He gives only good gifts.[40]

Even when times are hard, we can rest in the understanding that the season we are in is not an accident. It is the hand of God working to bring about something beautiful and wonderful in our lives.

David and Moses had plenty of experience with the wilderness, and whenever they hit difficult times, they both sought to saturate themselves with the lovingkindness of God. They maintained their contentment in the wilderness by "feeding" on God's nature and character:

> *"But as for me, I shall sing of Your strength;*
> *Yes, I shall joyfully sing of Your lovingkindness in the*
> *morning, For You have been my stronghold*
> *And a refuge in the day of my distress."*   — Psalm 59:16

> *"Because Your lovingkindness is better than life,*
> *My lips will praise You."*   — Psalm 63:3

> *"To declare Your lovingkindness in the morning*
> *And Your faithfulness by night . . . "*   — Psalm 92:2

> *"I will sing of lovingkindness and justice,*
> *To You, O Lord, I will sing praises."*   — Psalm 101:1

I love Psalm 90:14, where Moses sought to soak himself in God's lovingkindness, so he could sing for joy and be glad all his days. That is being full of God. That is being content.

In the wilderness, gaining and then maintaining a heart of contentment is one of the principle forces that thrusts us into God's plan for our victory and blessing. When we are filled with Jesus, knowing that He is working something great in our lives, contentment permeates our souls and sets us free from lust and covetousness, which are the opposite of contentment.

In the wilderness, Jesus declared to the devil, *"Man shall not live on bread alone, but on every word that proceeds out of the mouth of God"* (Matthew 4:4). The "manna" of our Father's voice is enough for our continued existence. In a wilderness of transition, we need to hold on to an attitude of contentment, allowing ourselves to be filled to overflowing with the greatness of Jesus. Contentment means being saturated with the fullness of the Lord.

An Attitude of Truth

What I call an attitude of truth is a mindset that is focused on and continuously declares the truth of God. An attitude of truth enables us to face adverse situations well, keeping our minds on God's assessment of our circumstances, not our own. An attitude of truth also helps us reject any lies that try to enter our hearts and minds.

When the nation of Israel encountered a trial, they began to confess lies about God's character and about themselves as His people.[41] They did not accept His truth concerning their destiny and ability in Him. In Numbers 14:3 they cried, *"Why is the Lord bringing us into this land, to fall by the sword? Our wives and our little ones will become plunder; would it not be better for us to return to Egypt?"* They panicked — when there was no reason for them to panic. If they had only believed the truth, they would have been able to stand in victory.

An attitude of truth is what allowed Joshua and Caleb to go into the Promised Land. When they faced an obstacle, they didn't cower in fear and join the rest of the people in their complaints. Instead, they declared the truth of God:

> *"Joshua the son of Nun and Caleb the son of Jephunneh, of those who had spied out the land, tore their clothes; and they spoke to all the congregation of the sons of Israel, saying, 'The land which we passed through to spy out is an exceedingly good land. If the Lord is pleased with us, then He will bring us into this land and give it to us — a land which flows*

with milk and honey. Only do not rebel against the Lord; and do not fear the people of the land, for they will be our prey. Their protection has been removed from them, and the Lord is with us; do not fear them.'" — Numbers 14:6–9

Whenever David faced a trial, he ran to the Lord for counsel. He strengthened himself in God:

"Moreover David was greatly distressed because the people spoke of stoning him, for all the people were embittered, each one because of his sons and his daughters. But David strengthened himself in the Lord his God. Then David said to Abiathar the priest, the son of Ahimelech, 'Please bring me the ephod.' So Abiathar brought the ephod to David. David inquired of the Lord, saying, 'Shall I pursue this band? Shall I overtake them?'" — 1 Samuel 30:6–8

An attitude of truth means we can see the situation from Heaven's perspective, even during seasons of uncertainty. This attitude enabled David to be the great king he was. It enabled Joshua and Caleb to stand strong against the tide of the masses.

I once observed a woman making a picture on fabric with needlepoint. She meticulously worked her needle with threads of various colors back and forth through the fabric. The interesting thing to me was that as I looked at the picture from the top, I could see it was a beautiful work of art. But when I looked at the underside of the fabric, it was confusing and distorted. I actually wondered, How could something so beautiful on the top look so bad on the bottom?

Then it hit me. That is just what life on earth is like. When we look at life from the bottom, from earth's perspective, it often looks ugly, distorted, and confusing. But when we can get Heaven's perspective, life becomes beautiful and meaningful. Heaven's perspective is the attitude of truth. We have to choose to see things from Heaven's perspective so we can maintain the right attitude.

An Attitude of Faith

In a wilderness of transition, the next important principle to remember is an attitude of faith. We cannot allow ourselves to be distracted by the "facts" and circumstances surrounding us. Instead, we need to focus on God's Word and character. Many times in the wilderness of transition, things will begin to look hopeless. We start wondering, What am I going to do? How am I going to provide for my family? Maybe taking this job or moving to this city wasn't a good idea. However, when we refuse to allow our circumstances to alter our faith, God will work on our behalf, and confidence and hope will be established in our hearts.

Unbelief, the opposite of faith, was a major contributor to the way Israel faltered in the wilderness:

> *"And with whom was He angry for forty years? Was it not with those who sinned, whose bodies fell in the wilderness? And to whom did He swear that they would not enter His rest, but to those who were disobedient? So we see that they were not able to enter because of unbelief."*
> — Hebrews 3:17–19

Most of Abraham's life was a wilderness of transition. "With respect to the promise of God," he held strongly to his faith, and this enabled him to receive all that God had prepared for him.[42] By the end of his life, he was utterly convinced that the Lord was the fulfiller of all needs and promises.

In the wilderness of transition, God is working to establish a word He planted in our hearts. It is very important that we hold fast to that word, believing it is true, because the word is the reason for the wilderness. We are in the wilderness because of the word. At the right time, just as He did with Abraham, Joseph, and David, the Lord will bring us out of the wilderness and establish the reality of His promise.

We Are God's Letter

"I will put My laws into their minds,
And I will write them on their hearts.
And I will be their God,
And they shall be My people."

— Hebrews 8:10

Our lives are letters to those we love. We are testimonies of God's goodness. He is writing a beautiful story in our hearts, and as people "read" this story, it empowers and inspires them to live life to its fullest. If everything around us were a constant tone or brightness, the fullness of beauty could not be seen. We need contrast. In the wilderness God writes into our hearts a value and appreciation for both the small and large things in life. He doesn't write His best stuff in our hearts during the good times, because in the good times, our hearts usually are not open to such revelations. It is in the contrast of a wilderness that some of God's best writing occurs.

Whenever we find ourselves in a wilderness, God is seeking to do a work in our hearts that establishes His laws, character, and ways within us. The wilderness is our opportunity, and our responsibility, to participate with Him by expressing His truth with our words and actions. We release outwardly the character of what He is doing inside us, displaying His truth back to Him through our love and affection for Him. We reveal His truth to others as we encourage and empower them.

When I read in Scripture that God's lovingkindness is better than life, I am benefited; that is a good truth to know. But when I understand that David wrote those words in the contrast of a wilderness, the truth becomes beautiful.

We want to partner with God in the work of art He is creating. Inspired by the Holy Spirit, Paul wrote, *"Work out your salvation with fear and trembling; for it is God who is at work in you, both to will and to work for His good pleasure"* (Philippians 2:12–13). If God says that a woman will be a warrior in the spirit realm, and she then finds herself facing opposition, she needs to allow her character to be formed into that of a warrior. If the Lord declares a man will have provision or wealth, and that man finds himself in a position of lack, he needs to allow dependency on God to be established in his heart. It is in the contrast of the wilderness that the beauty and greatness of God are established in our hearts. In a wilderness of transition, we work with God to build the character of His word within us.

God in the Wilderness

In summary, we enter a wilderness of transition when God is bringing us into a new realm of authority, gifting, blessing, or ministry. The wilderness of transition has an amazing purpose in that God is working within us to bring about our destinies.

The purpose of this wilderness is to test a word God has spoken and establish the character necessary for that word in our hearts. We come out of this wilderness with hearts of humility, having a proper perspective of ourselves. We are completely dependent on God and have a better understanding of how the Body of Christ is meant to operate. As a result of our newfound humility and the word being established in our hearts, we are empowered and exalted by God into the destinies He has prepared for us.

How do we recognize when we are in a wilderness of transition? One way is that we heard a word of direction from the Lord a short time before we entered this season. We can also know we are in a wilderness of transition because we started something new or the Lord told us the season was coming. This wilderness is not a time of punishment but of preparation for promotion.

Whenever we find ourselves in a wilderness of transition, we want to respond in a way that launches us into the destinies God has prepared. We can rejoice and thank Him, knowing something great is ahead of us. It is also important to walk in contentment. This enables us to extract truths from the Lord, adding them to the fabric of our lives. When we are content, we can be patient, not rushing ahead of the Lord's timing. Fostering an attitude of truth and faith empowers our contentment in the wilderness season and enables us to step into the destinies the Lord has for us at the right time.

God is doing a great work in you. With your life, He is writing a letter that will affect the lives of those around you:

> *"You are a letter of Christ, cared for by us, written not with ink but with the Spirit of the living God, not on tablets of stone but on tablets of human hearts. Such confidence we have through Christ toward God. Not that we are adequate in ourselves to consider anything as coming from ourselves, but our adequacy is from God."* — 2 Corinthians 3:3–5

In the wilderness, we come to depend on God. We realize that He is everything to us, and our adequacy is from Him.

Notes / Reference Scriptures

A. It is so important to have your needs met in Jesus. You can learn more about needs in my book entitled - *Jesus: The Filler of Needs*. For more information, visit dealingjesus.org.

1. Numbers 11:4-5
2. Exodus 17:3
3. Joshua 5:6
4. Numbers 14:1-2
5. Exodus 15:22
6. Genesis 12:1-3
7. Genesis 12:10
8. John 21:2-3
9. Acts 3:12, 16
10. Proverbs 30:5
11. Matthew 4:1
12. Luke 4:1
13. Luke 4:14
14. Romans 4:12-16
15. Romans 8:29
16. Matthew 28:19;
    2 Corinthians 5:18-20
17. 1 Thessalonians 2:8
18. 1 Corinthians 4:1-2
19. Deuteronomy 8:2
20. Matthew 4:1
21. Matthew 13:19
22. 1 Corinthians 10:13
23. Romans 5:3-5
24. James 1:2-4
25. Hebrews 11:17
26. James 2:21-22
27. Deuteronomy 8:12-14
28. 1 Peter 5:6
29. Psalm 25:9, 12
30. Philippians 2:12-13
31. Genesis 12:1-10
32. Psalm 63:1-3
33. Nehemiah 8:10
34. Acts 7:39
35. Jeremiah 31:3
36. Hebrews 13:5-6
37. Psalm 37:23-24
38. 1 Thessalonians 5:24
39. John 17:22
40. James 1:16-17
41. Exodus 16:3
42. Romans 4:17-20

6   The Wilderness of Sin and Death

In 1995 I was heavily involved in ministering on the campuses of Virginia Tech and Radford University. God was doing an amazing work, and we were seeing students saved and set free.

But in the midst of this revival, the church I had left back in 1991 was going through a tough time. I felt guilty for leaving those precious people behind, and the guilt grew in my heart until I eventually left the flourishing ministries at Tech and Radford. I didn't listen to the Lord, and with a savior mentality gripping my heart, I returned to the church I had pastored.

But as I got back into the flow of things at that church, it became apparent that the Holy Spirit wasn't empowering and blessing my ministry. I would preach good material—I knew it was good, but it would somehow come out disorganized and convoluted, like I was preaching in a fog. Even Paula would stare at me with a look that asked, "What are you saying?" I had to have two surgeries during this time, and I developed a mild heart condition due to stress. Paula had to have surgery as well, and we started losing Shea in his walk with the Lord. It was a very dark time for us.

Late one Sunday night when I was praying about the fruitlessness of my ministry and the hardships we were going through, the Lord spoke very clearly to me. He said I had come back to the church in sin. I was shocked and asked how that was possible. He reminded me of how my return to the church had transpired and that I hadn't listened to Him. So I did the only thing I knew to do. I repented. I resigned again from that precious church and caused them pain. I found myself in a dark time of depression, believing I was totally washed up as a minister of the Gospel due to my unfaithfulness. The wilderness for me was deep and intense.

But God, being rich in mercy, started speaking to me about His lovingkindness and faithfulness. He lovingly led us to Boone, North Carolina, to enter a time of restoration and healing. Paula started teaching again, this time in the excellent Christian school Shea and Michele attended; Shea was one of her students. A friend was a campus minister at Appalachian State, and I became his assistant and helped minister in the church that was overseeing the campus ministry. God restored us to health and eventually sent us out from that church to start a church on the campus of Virginia Tech, returning us to the ministry we had left years before.

The wilderness I experienced during that time of hardship was a wilderness of sin and death. We don't enter this wilderness because it is God's will for our lives; we are led into this type of wilderness by our thoughts, words, and actions. Specifically, the wilderness of sin and death occurs for three main reasons.

The first is that we were disobedient to a word we received from the Lord. When the Lord spoke to Jonah about going to Nineveh and instead he boarded a boat to go to Tarshish, the prophet entered a wilderness of sin and death. The story I just told you from my own life is another example. I was disobedient to a word I received from the Lord; therefore, I went into a season when I needed God's restorative mercy and grace to heal me. God speaks into our lives and gives us revelation concerning where we can find His life and provisions. When we go where God has not provided life and provisions, the natural result is sin and death. But praise God—He always plans ways to help us and works to bring the lost ones home.

The second way we enter this wilderness is when we have established something, someone, or even a place other than Jesus Christ as the fulfiller of our needs. While in Egypt, Israel developed a slave mindset, and they looked to the Egyptians to satisfy their needs,[1] instead of looking to God. They also had a mindset that was idolatrous and immoral.[2] When we are convinced that something is our source of fulfillment, we will listen to that voice and long for it in our hearts. The result of longing for something to meet our needs other than Jesus and His will is sin, rebellion, and worldly indulgence. Our Father is holy, righteous, and just, and He cannot participate or have relationship with unrighteousness or unholiness.[3] When we hold on to our sin, it severely hinders our ability to hear and receive the Lord's care, direction, and provisions.

But our Father doesn't want to lose us. He makes plans so *"the banished one will not be cast out from Him"* (2 Samuel 14:14). He longs to draw us to Himself. He works and plans ways we can repent and walk in the purposes He prepared for us. And then, as we walk in His plans and purposes, we experience the depth of His goodness.

The third way we can enter the wilderness of sin and death is when we squander God's blessings and provisions on worldly desires. We see this clearly in Jesus' story of the prodigal son, who used his father's resources on unwholesome pursuits and activities that "impoverished" him:

> *"A man had two sons. The younger of them said to his father, 'Father, give me the share of the estate that falls to me.' So he divided his wealth between them. And not many days later, the younger son gathered everything together and went on a journey into a distant country, and there he squandered his estate with loose living. Now when he had spent everything, a severe famine occurred in that country, and he began to be impoverished."* — Luke 15:11–14

The wilderness of sin and death occurs because of the principle of sowing and reaping. Whatever we sow we will reap. If we invest in our flesh, we will reap the flesh, but if we invest in the Spirit of God, we will reap eternal life.[4]

As children of God, we can know His heart. He longs for us to know Him well and walk in His ways, as He expressed in Psalm 81:10–14:

"I, the Lord, am your God,
Who brought you up from the land of Egypt;
Open your mouth wide and I will fill it.
But My people did not listen to My voice,
And Israel did not obey Me.
So I gave them over to the stubbornness of their heart,
To walk in their own devices.
Oh that My people would listen to Me,
That Israel would walk in My ways!
I would quickly subdue their enemies
And turn My hand against their adversaries."

Do you see God's heart in this passage? He wants us to have life, but if we hold on to sin and death, He must legally give us what we want. As Psalm 81 states, the people were yearning for what would ultimately kill them (their sinful ways), and God gave them what they wanted. The father in the parable of the prodigal son didn't lead his son into the wilderness of sin and death. He didn't put him there. The son took the action himself, and the father allowed him to pursue his desires. That is the same thing God did with Israel.

As we investigate the wilderness of sin and death, we continually need to remember two truths. First, God does not vary in giving good gifts.[5] His gifts are always good. And second, He is the only One who can satisfy our needs. When we focus on anything other than Jesus to satisfy our hungers and thirsts, it brings about some form of death in our lives.

Examples of Sin and Death

Let's look at three examples of the wilderness of sin and death found in Scripture.

Israel Wandering in the Desert

> *"'But as for you, your corpses will fall in this wilderness. Your sons shall be shepherds for forty years in the wilderness, and they will suffer for your unfaithfulness, until your corpses lie in the wilderness.'"* — Numbers 14:32–33

The children of Israel experienced a wilderness that lasted forty years after they refused to enter the Promised Land. Two different types of wildernesses occurred simultaneously. For the men of fighting age who came out of Egypt, it was a wilderness of sin and death because of their disobedience. For the children of Israel (those aged nineteen and younger when they left Egypt, as well as those born in the desert), it was a wilderness of transition that prepared them for the Promised Land.

I knew a pastor who experienced an incredible amount of heartache. He felt his ministry was fruitless, and life's disappointments injured his soul. He ended up doing what the Israelites did—he turned from God and his call and entered a wilderness of sin and death. Holding to his bitterness, he became an alcoholic in an effort to numb the pain. A long time passed for him in this wilderness, but his daughter finally was able to get through to him, and he left the wilderness behind. God's love restores us. Always, every time.

Gomer, Hosea's Wife

> *"Therefore, behold, I will allure her,*
> *Bring her into the wilderness And speak kindly to her.*
> *Then I will give her her vineyards from there,*
> *And the valley of Achor as a door of hope.*
> *And she will sing there as in the days of her youth,*
> *As in the day when she came up from the land of Egypt."*
> — Hosea 2:14–15

Hosea married a prostitute who was unfaithful to him. Gomer believed it was her lovers who met her needs, so she was deceived and lured into a wilderness of sin and death.[6] Keep in mind that Gomer's story represented the unfaithfulness of Israel and Judah during the time of the kings. She was portraying the sin of an entire people with her lifestyle and choices.

When I left a thriving ministry to go back to the church I had pastored before, the real reason for my return was the state of my heart. I wasn't going to God to have my needs met. I was looking to brothers and sisters instead and craving the love and acceptance of other people, which thrust me into a time of wilderness. But when I repented and sought God to meet my needs, He lovingly restored my heart and ministry.

The Man in 1 Corinthians 5

"It is actually reported that there is immorality among you, and immorality of such a kind as does not exist even among the Gentiles, that someone has his father's wife. You have become arrogant and have not mourned instead, so that the one who had done this deed would be removed from your midst. For I, on my part, though absent in body but present in spirit, have already judged him who has so committed this, as though I were present. In the name of our Lord Jesus, when you are assembled, and I with you in spirit, with the power of our Lord Jesus, I have decided to deliver such a one to Satan for the destruction of his flesh, so that his spirit may be saved in the day of the Lord Jesus."

— 1 Corinthians 5:1–5

Paul turned this man over to Satan for the "destruction of his flesh." The man entered a wilderness of sin and death — so he could be saved from death. The wilderness was going to destroy his fleshly desires and, in the end, produce life within him.

I know a man of God who had unmet needs but refused to allow the Lord to minister to the depths of his heart. Instead, he turned to pornography and sexual immorality to sedate the pain, and he found himself in a similar situation as the man in 1 Corinthians 5. The wilderness of sin and death is hard to endure. It is a difficult road through a difficult land, but as the prodigal son experienced, in the wilderness we come to our senses.

When we fill our hearts with anything other than the Lord, the natural effects of sin and death will eventually take place. In Scripture the word death implies separation and decay, and we can see this as the effects of our sin occur; we are separated from the flow of life found in God. It is not good to be in a state of sin and not realize what is happening, and in a wilderness of sin and death, we have the opportunity to come to our senses and deal with the issues that released the effects of death in our lives.

God's Heart in a Wilderness of Sin and Death

In the Eagle's Nest Regeneration Program at our church, we continually meet men who turned to substance abuse and threw themselves headfirst into a wilderness of sin and death. As the consequences of addiction materialized, these men were drawn into lifestyles that spiraled deeper and deeper into the effects of death. They lost their jobs, businesses, and families. But it always amazes me to see God's hand working in their lives to bring them back into His goodness and restore them completely.

God is good, and He gives only good gifts. Therefore, in the wilderness of sin and death, He is acting with a good purpose. He is trying to remove the things in our hearts the devil uses to entice us toward death. The enemy wants to see us wandering in death and heartache until the day we physically die, but God, rich in kindness, does not give up on us. Over and over again, He will seek to redeem our lives. If He did not go after the issues that led us into the wilderness in the first place, we wouldn't be able to find true freedom. We would eventually end up right where we started, headed back into the wilderness.

Separated from Deception and Temptation

The deceitfulness of sin is one of the main reasons we find ourselves in a wilderness of sin and death. The devil is powerful in his ability to deceive us, and the goal of his deception is to make us run to anyone other than Jesus, fleeing the relationships and callings we are purposed for.

> *"For their mother has played the harlot;*
> *She who conceived them has acted shamefully.*
> *For she said, 'I will go after my lovers,*
> *Who give me my bread and my water,*
> *My wool and my flax, my oil and my drink.'*
> *Therefore, behold,* **I will hedge up her way with thorns,**
> **And I will build a wall against her so that she cannot**
> **find her paths.** *She will pursue her lovers, but she will not*
> *overtake them; And she will seek them, but will not find*
> *them."* — Hosea 2:5–7 (emphasis added)

We need Jesus. That is the simple truth. We were made in such a way that He is the only One who can meet our needs. He is the key for all creation, so when He is not our Source, we run into some problems—namely, our unfulfilled needs take over and begin to dictate our choices and actions. In the world, what is thought to be fulfillment is actually a trap for sin and death. Whenever we attempt to have our needs met outside of Christ, we will eventually find ourselves struggling in the enemy's snare, captured by deception.

In His love and mercy, God allows us to enter a wilderness of sin and death so we can be set free from bondage. Sometimes we cannot see clearly enough to break free from sin on our own, so we first have to be separated from the sin or the source of what is negatively influencing us. Then we can see the truth. God is the One who causes all things to work out for our good. He can take a wilderness we have caused and turn it into a positive thing.

In the wilderness of sin and death, we are separated from the deceptions that held us captive. As the separation occurs,

God works in our hearts, and we can come to our senses. We *"escape from the snare of the devil, having been help captive by him to do his will"* (2 Timothy 2:26).

God's Judgment Brings Life

Our heavenly Father is full of grace, kindness, and love, but He is also the God of absolute justice and righteousness. He judges our lives at two different times. There is the final judgment that all of us will face at the end of the age,[7] when the full effects of our lives will be examined and we are rewarded according to our actions.[8] But another time of judgment is going on in the courtroom of Heaven right now.[9] The purpose of the current judgment is that we would learn righteousness and not be condemned in the final judgment:

> *"At night my soul longs for You,*
> *Indeed, my spirit within me seeks You diligently;*
> *For when the earth experiences Your judgments*
> *The inhabitants of the world learn righteousness."*
> — Isaiah 26:9

> *"But when we are judged, we are disciplined by the Lord so that we will not be condemned along with the world."*
> — 1 Corinthians 11:32

This judgment occurs now, in our lifetimes, so we have the opportunity to deal with the sin and other issues that could cause us to suffer loss.[10] Many times, the wilderness of sin and death is the outflow of justice being brought to pass in our lives. We did something that was wrong, and we are now experiencing the consequences.

In the following passage, it is clear that Israel was holding on to unhealthy things—but God didn't force the people to change their ways. Instead, He judicially gave them over to the lust of their hearts:

113

"But My people did not listen to My voice,
And Israel did not obey Me.
So I gave them over to the stubbornness of their heart,
To walk in their own devices."   — Psalm 81:11–12

God is just. When we decide to keep sinning, He turns us over to those decisions. We are legally choosing sin; therefore, we legally get sin and its effects in our lives. But the same God who judges in justice and righteousness also judges in loving-kindness and faithfulness,[11] and He works to bring us back to Himself. We experience the fullness of His lovingkindness only after we have gained in the wilderness the revelation that sin is death and we were created for abundant life.

Exposed Because of Love

Our sin is exposed in this wilderness. That may sound harsh, but it isn't meant to be harsh—it is a deep expression of love.

"Or I will strip her naked
And expose her as on the day when she was born.
I will also make her like a wilderness,
Make her like desert land
And slay her with thirst . . .
And then I will uncover her lewdness
In the sight of her lovers,
And no one will rescue her out of My hand."
                                                        — Hosea 2:3, 10

When we are deceived and in sin, the worst thing that could happen to us would be staying in the deception. In His tough love and mercy, God does not enable us in our sin. He removes His covering, so we can start to perceive our sin and, there-fore, our need for a Savior. Paul wrote about this in 2 Timothy 2:24–26:

"The Lord's bond-servant must not be quarrelsome, but
be kind to all, able to teach, patient when wronged, with

gentleness correcting those who are in opposition, if perhaps God may grant them repentance leading to the knowledge of the truth, and they may come to their senses and escape from the snare of the devil, having been held captive by him to do his will."

The wages of sin is death, and if our sin isn't dealt with, our lives will eventually fall apart; we will experience the wages of the sin we have embraced.

Redemption of the Heart

A wilderness of sin and death can be a harsh place, for the effects of sin are harsh; they lead to death. At times God's redemption process can seem harsh as well, but He is working to bring us life.

The Hebrew men of war had destructive mindsets that released painful realities into their existence:

> *"For the sons of Israel walked forty years in the wilderness, until all the nation, that is, the men of war who came out of Egypt, perished because they did not listen to the voice of the Lord, to whom the Lord had sworn that He would not let them see the land which the Lord had sworn to their fathers to give us, a land flowing with milk and honey."*
>
> — Joshua 5:6

When we read a passage like this, it is important to remember that the Old Testament was written as an example for us.[12] So out of Joshua 5:6, we can extrapolate that God leads us into the wilderness in order for the sin in our hearts to die—or more accurately, so we can come into agreement with the finished work of the Cross. The men of Israel "did not listen to the voice of the Lord." Instead of agreeing with God to conquer the obstacles before them, they wanted to quit and go back to Egypt, where it was "safe." As He allowed the men of war to die off, in a way God was purging His people and getting rid of their sin.

Israel's journey into the Promised Land mirrors our individual walks with the Lord. Every city and area they had to conquer is a metaphor for the areas in our hearts that need to agree with God and come under His reign. Most of us could find places in our hearts that correspond to what the Hebrew men of war struggled with. We don't always want to fight the "giants" in our lives to walk in faith[13] and believe God for His salvation, but those areas need to come into agreement with the finished work of the Cross. This process is called renewing the mind. One of the most important aspects of renewing the mind is setting apart Christ as the Lord of our hearts.[14]

Obviously, God's heart is not to kill us when we make mistakes or sin in some way. He does, however, want our hearts to be dead to sin and alive to Him.[15] Jesus died for our sins once and for all. When we accept Him as our Lord and Savior, and identify with His death and burial through water baptism, the work of God is established in us.[16] Our old selves have been rendered powerless.[17] We have been crucified with Christ, yet it is possible to have areas in our hearts that haven't yet come into agreement with the spiritual reality of the Cross.

When I left the Blacksburg area to go back to my first pastorate, I entered the wilderness because areas in my heart thought like Israel's men of war. I became focused on what had happened in the past; I wanted to re-experience the past more than I wanted to have faith for the uncertainties of the future. I carried a lot of guilt and had difficulty embracing God's mercy and grace. I also had a few wrong assumptions about the Holy Spirit and revival. Somewhere in the back of my mind, I was thinking He would do what I wanted Him to do on command, as if He were my servant and not the other way around. Part of me believed I was the "savior" for our old church, but there is only one Savior and it sure isn't me! My mindset had to come into agreement with God's truth. As I walked through the wilderness of sin and death—right where my destructive thinking had brought me—those problem areas in my heart died off.

When we enter a wilderness of sin and death because of an area of sin in our lives, it is an opportunity for God to change us, heal us, draw us closer to Him, and remove the sin that is trying to harm us. His redemption is established in our hearts. In the wilderness I started discovering that with Jesus, the uncertainties of the future are far more secure than trying to live in the past. I learned to treasure every move of God no matter its size and trust in His mercy and grace to redeem my mistakes.

And as simple as it sounds, I also learned that Jesus is Jesus and I need Him as my Savior—He doesn't need me to be a savior. In retrospect, I can see that I entered the wilderness because of God's mercy and grace. He loves me too much to allow me to walk through life with areas of my heart filled with lies and crippling thought processes. When I gained the revelation I needed, He was there to take me by the hand and lovingly bring me out of the wilderness, saying with His every action, "Let's try this again."

Gain a God-Seeking Heart

Once we are separated from the deceptions that would harm us, the wilderness of sin and death helps us reestablish Jesus as our Lover, Savior, Redeemer, and conquering King. When Gomer and the nation of Israel first entered the wilderness, both depended on someone or something other than God to be the source of their fulfillment:

> *"Then she will say, 'I will go back to my first husband, For it was better for me then than now!'"*   — Hosea 2:7

Every time we sin, God's heart is that we would come back to Him. When we are separated from the deceptions of sin and the world, we start to see clearly again, and our hearts want to return to the pure and simple love of God.

The prodigal son gained this type of heart when he lost everything and found himself feeding pigs:

> *"And he would have gladly filled his stomach with the pods that the swine were eating, and no one was giving anything to him. But when he came to his senses, he said, 'How many of my father's hired men have more than enough bread, but I am dying here with hunger! I will get up and go to my father, and will say to him, "Father, I have sinned against*

heaven, and in your sight; I am no longer worthy to be called your son; make me as one of your hired men."' So he got up and came to his father. But while he was still a long way off, his father saw him and felt compassion for him, and ran and embraced him and kissed him."   — Luke 15:16–20

In the wilderness of sin and death, the son realized what he needed: He needed to be with his father. The wilderness of sin and death can help us realize what is truly important, what we really need. We come to understand that what we are holding on to is not bringing us life, and like the prodigal son, we suddenly see that the place we want to be is with our Father. We have a sure promise from God: The one who hungers and thirsts for righteousness will be filled.[23]

Hear God's Voice

Gomer, Hosea's wife, was dying in her sin. God told Hosea He was going to bring Gomer (who represented Israel) into a wilderness in order to do two things: to separate her from her sin and reveal sweet things to her — that is, He wanted to show her His heart:

> *"Therefore, behold, I will allure her, Bring her into the wilderness And speak kindly to her.*
> *Then I will give her her vineyards from there,*
> *And the valley of Achor as a door of hope.*
> *And she will sing there as in the days of her youth,*
> *As in the day when she came up from the land of Egypt."*
>   — Hosea 2:14–15

The wilderness of sin and death is the opportunity for us to rediscover life. We are separated from the voices of the world and our flesh so we can begin to hear God's voice again, which is crucial to our walk with Him:

> *"When he puts forth all his own, he goes ahead of them, and the sheep follow him because they know his voice. A*

stranger they simply will not follow, but will flee from him, because they do not know the voice of strangers."

— John 10:4–5

We follow the Lord because we know His voice. We don't get distracted with counterfeit lovers, because we don't "know" them. If we don't know the voice of God, how will we be able to walk in victory? Before the wilderness, the voice of the deceiver can easily distract us from the voice of our true love and Lord. But in the wilderness of sin and death, we have the opportunity to recalibrate our discernment.

The Lord's heart is that the "valley of Achor" (the valley of trouble) would be a doorway to our restoration. The wilderness of sin and death can be a tough thing to experience—but restoration and life are the result.

Throughout Scripture, it is easy to see God's desire to bring His people back to Himself. Righteousness and justice are the foundational principles in everything He does. He works to expose sin, separate us from sin (and the influences that cause us to sin), and bring our hearts back to Him. He does these things so we can experience His goodness and lovingkindness. He constantly reveals His goodness to us, because it is His goodness that leads us to repentance.[18]

A key to redemption in the wilderness of sin and death is realizing our Father's heart. We love because He first loved us. As we begin to grasp the revelations of His heart of love and how He longs for us, we will be able to respond to Him appropriately.

"Therefore the Lord longs to be gracious to you,
And therefore He waits on high to have compassion on you.
For the Lord is a God of justice;
How blessed are all those who long for Him.
O people in Zion, inhabitant in Jerusalem, you will weep no longer. He will surely be gracious to you at the sound of your cry; when He hears it, He will answer you."

— Isaiah 30:18–19

We can be confident in the knowledge that our Father does what He does in order to save us, so we can come out of death and into life.

Responding in the Wilderness of Sin and Death

What should we do when we realize we are in a wilderness because of our sin? All we have to do is repent, confess our sin, and do what God told us to do. These responses open doorways of life. They lead us out of the wilderness and reset the direction of our lives.

Repentance

Repentance is from the Greek word metanoia, which means "another mind." In other words, when we come to a place of repentance, our thinking literally changes. Every wilderness of sin and death is the result of a conclusion in our hearts and minds that is leading us astray. Paul wrote in Romans 14:22 that what we choose to believe is our conviction before God. He added, *"Happy is he who does not condemn himself in what he approves."* (that is, in what he chooses to believe). We enter a wilderness of sin and death because what we have chosen to believe is bringing death into our lives. But in the process of repentance, we come to understand that we need to think in a different way.

I have dear friends who chose to believe that certain sinful lifestyles were acceptable, and after a while, they began to experience measures of death because of those choices. What they chose to believe was released into their lives, and they condemned themselves in their beliefs, as Paul wrote. But when they repented, everything changed. They realigned themselves with the Lord's way, and He released abundant blessing upon them.

When we willfully sin, the Lord often turns us over to our own devices. What we think we want is allowed to bring into our lives what we actually do not want. Our sin separates us from the Lord's presence and provision, and in that area of our lives, we enter a time of wilderness. That area will stay in the wilderness of sin and death until the sin we are holding on to dies in our hearts.

Once we surrender the area of sin, we experience the Lord's refreshing: *"Therefore repent and return, so that your sins may be wiped away, in order that times of refreshing may come from the presence of the Lord"* (Acts 3:19). We can throw ourselves into the life and freedom our Father offers us.

When we realize we have been walking in an area of death, it is common to feel sorrow, but sorrow is good only if it is coupled with God's character; if the sorrow is not directed toward God's character, it can bring death:

> *"For the sorrow that is according to the will of God produces a repentance without regret, leading to salvation, but the sorrow of the world produces death. For behold what earnestness this very thing, this godly sorrow, has produced in you: what vindication of yourselves, what indignation, what fear, what longing, what zeal, what avenging of wrong! In everything you demonstrated yourselves to be innocent in the matter."* — 2 Corinthians 7:10–11

Worldly sorrow produces death and draws us into guilt and condemnation. Godly sorrow, on the other hand, produces repentance that doesn't seek to justify itself or express anger or vengeance. When a heart is filled with godly sorrow and repentance, the person just wants to return to God. He or she wants Jesus. That attitude is important in order to come out of this wilderness. In the story of the prodigal son, the young man realized the futility of an ungodly life. He repented in his wilderness — meaning, he had "another mind" or way of thinking about his source of life. His repentant attitude compelled him to return to his father's house at all costs. He did not care if he had to work as a servant; he just wanted to be in the father's house.

Confession of Sin

As we come to the point of repentance, it is important to confess the sin that brought us into the wilderness. When the prodigal son came home, the first thing he did was ask for forgiveness from his father.[19] When we confess our sins, we can know without a shadow of doubt that they are forgiven and cleansed.[20]

When our sins have affected others, it is good to confess them to those people.[21] James tells us to confess our sins to one another and pray for one another *so that you may be healed* (James 5:16). Sometimes we need a faithful brother or sister to agree with us in our forgiveness and stand with us in restoration. This is not anything fancy; it is simply asking a brother or sister (depending on your gender) to pray with you as you confess things to the Lord.

A Heart of Obedience

Obedience is a natural overflow of repentance and confession of sin. In the New Testament, the Greek word for "obedience" is hupakouo, which means "to hear under."[22] When we are obedient to the Lord, we are responding positively to His promptings and guidance. In most cases, it is a heart of disobedience that leads us into the wilderness of sin and death. We want to do our own thing, in our own way, and we aren't willing to be led by Jesus.

Look at what God said in Psalm 81:11–14:

> *"But My people did not listen to My voice,*
> *And Israel did not obey Me.*
> *So I gave them over to the stubbornness of their heart,*
> *To walk in their own devices.*
> *Oh, that My people would listen to Me,*
> *That Israel would walk in My ways!*
> *I would quickly subdue their enemies*
> *And turn My hand against their adversaries."*

If disobedience got us into the wilderness, it only makes sense that obedience will get us out! Notice what else God declared in Psalm 81—if we listen to Him, He will quickly deal with our enemies.

God in the Wilderness

The phrase wilderness of sin and death sounds ominous, but the simple truth is that anything that does not include God is sin and death, because He is life. The wilderness of sin and death is the result of choices and lifestyles we have entertained. Yet when we return to God, the season of death can actually become a season of redemption.

In the wilderness of sin and death, God's heart is to bring us to Himself. Every characteristic of His heart has at its root the pulse of a loving heavenly Father who wants to see His children find life. From His perspective, the wilderness of sin and death is a time of redemption, so the ones who have wandered from the path of life can find restoration. He works to separate us from deception and temptation, and His judgment means exercising His fatherly discipline to bring life. Our sin is exposed so our hearts can experience His healing. We gain God-seeking hearts that long to hear His voice.

We can find ourselves in a wilderness of sin and death for one of three reasons:

1. We were disobedient to a word from the Lord.
2. We have set our hearts on someone or something other than God to be the supplier of our needs.
3. We squandered the Lord's resources and provisions.

Whenever we find ourselves in this wilderness, three simple responses can bring us out again:

1. Repentance, which means taking on another mind or way of thinking;

2. Confessing the sin we entertained that put us in the wilderness in the first place; and

3. Taking on a heart of obedience, where we become willing to do whatever the Lord is asking us to do.

The thing to keep in mind is that God is the God of redemption. He is working to cause all situations and circumstances to turn out for our good—even the wilderness of sin and death. This wilderness can be a difficult thing to experience, but the Lord is faithful, and He has redemption ready and waiting.

Notes / Reference Scriptures

1. Numbers 11:4-5
2. 1 Corinthians 10:1-8
3. 2 Chronicles 19:7
4. Galatians 6:7-8
5. James 1:16-17
6. Hosea 2:5
7. Hebrews 9:27
8. 1 Cornithians 4:5;
       2 Cornithians 5:10
9. Psalm 82:1
10. 1 Cornithians 3:14-15
11. Psalm 89:14

12. 1 Corinthians 10:11
13. Ephesians 3:17
14. 1 Peter 3:15
15. Romans 6:11
16. Galatians 2:20
17. Romans 6:6-7
18. Romans 2:4

19. Luke 15:21
20. 1 John 1:9
21. Matthew 5:23-24
22. Romans 6:17
23. Matthew 5:6

7 The Wilderness of Revelation

I once traveled to Beirut, Lebanon, during a time of political unrest. After I boarded the plane in Paris, a gentleman from Lebanon sat in the seat next to me. "Why are you going to Beirut?" he asked. "Don't you know it is dangerous?"

His words began to alarm me; I could feel fear trying to creep into my heart. But then I realized this was a setup from the enemy, meant to keep me from all God wanted to do on this trip, so I allowed my heart to pursue the security of the Lord instead of turning to fear.

It was an interesting trip for me. The instability in Lebanon would have been difficult enough, but I also wasn't feeling well. Many nights that week, I couldn't sleep because of the spiritual environment and because I felt so sick physically. Instead, I spent those sleepless hours discovering God's goodness and security. When I look back on that week, I realize it was one of the sweetest, most revealing times I've spent with God in my life. It pressed my faith into the realm of reality. I'm not saying I became this mighty, all-courageous man of God who had no fear, but during that season, I had a deep revelation of my need and desire for Him.

Many times when I travel overseas, it becomes a wilderness of revelation for me. A wilderness of revelation is a period of time we impose ourselves for the express purpose of receiving revelation from God. He might lead us into this wilderness, or we take ourselves into it on purpose, because we want to hear His voice. In a wilderness of revelation, we are separated from the support and comfort of the world. The world has many "voices" that try to distract us from what is truly important. The needs of our flesh and soul can hinder us from clearly hearing the voice of our heavenly Father. When we are set apart from the world, not allowing our fleshly and soulish needs to dominate our thinking, we can hear God much more easily. The wilderness of revelation brings us closer to Him, and in the quiet, we can hear Him.

> *"Therefore, behold, I will allure her,*
> *Bring her into the wilderness*
> *And speak kindly to her."* — Hosea 2:14

Examples of a Wilderness of Revelation

A wilderness of revelation is an important part of the Christian life, and every time it occurs, God's people are refreshed. We can find several examples of this wilderness in Scripture.

Receiving Revelation

After Paul became a Christian, he went into the Arabian wilderness for a time. He didn't go there to discover human counsel, but it was a time for the Lord to reveal Himself, His truth, and His purposes to Paul:

> *"But when God, who had set me apart even from my mother's womb and called me through His grace, was pleased to reveal His Son in me so that I might preach Him among the Gentiles, I did not immediately consult with flesh and blood, nor did I go up to Jerusalem to those who were apostles before me; but I went away to Arabia, and returned once more to Damascus."* — Galatians 1:15–17

Paul's time in the wilderness helped him understand the fullness of God's heart. Look at his response: *"The gospel which was preached by me is not according to man. For I neither received it from man, nor was I taught it, but I received it through a revelation of Jesus Christ"* (Galatians 1:11–12). Paul was separated from outside influences in a wilderness of revelation, and it enabled him to stand in faith on what he had received from the Lord. Sometimes the things of the Lord are so important for us that we need to be separated from everything else, so we can fully process what He is giving us.

The night before Jesus chose the twelve disciples, He separated Himself from the community to pray. He wanted to hear His Father. He did only what He saw the Father doing,[1] and He wanted to hear God's voice clearly so He could rightly choose the men who would walk alongside Him.[2]

> *"It was at this time that He went off to the mountain to pray, and He spent the whole night in prayer to God. And when day came, He called His disciples to Him and chose twelve of them, whom He also named as apostles."*
> — Luke 6:12–13

Jesus continually used the wilderness of revelation to seek His Father's will concerning what He was to say and do.

Revelation for Refreshment

> *"But the news about Him was spreading even farther, and large crowds were gathering to hear Him and to be healed of their sicknesses. But Jesus Himself would often slip away to the wilderness and pray."* — Luke 5:15–16

As Jesus' ministry grew, the pressure of people drawing on Him also grew. He would often go into a wilderness to pray; He would get away from the normal "flow" of life in order to refresh Himself with the presence of His Father, seeking the Father's heart. As I see Jesus relying on His Father in this manner, it inspires me to learn to do the same. If it was good for Jesus, the Son of the Most High God, it is most definitely good for me!

Revelation for Restoration

When King Herod had John the Baptist executed, it obviously grieved Jesus' heart. Jesus and John were cousins; they were family. The Word of God doesn't directly tell us that Jesus was hurting, but it does say that immediately after hearing the news, He sought to go into a wilderness or secluded place:

> *"His disciples came and took away the body and buried it; and they went and reported to Jesus. Now when Jesus heard about John, He withdrew from there in a boat to a secluded place by Himself; and when the people heard of this, they followed Him on foot from the cities."* — Matthew 14:12–13

It is interesting to note that the people followed Jesus, so He didn't immediately find the rest He wanted. But after He had fed the five thousand, He sent the disciples across the sea without Him, and He went off by Himself to pray.[3]

To speak simply, I cannot imagine being Jesus. When I think about His life from a human perspective, it is overwhelming. He knew He was going to have to carry all the sin, sickness, and abuse of every person who has ever existed. He saw and knew the pain of a world steeped in sin and death. I cannot help but wonder if, when He heard about John, the pain and suffering of this world really hit a tender and vulnerable spot within Him. I think He considered John a friend and they probably played together as kids. In response to John's death, Jesus needed to be with His Father, so His soul could be restored.[4]

Revelation of Love

In the following example, the wilderness was not a physical place but a time. The leaders of the church in Antioch set themselves apart to minister to the Lord. That was their purpose. They came together just to worship Him, and as a result, they were able to hear revelation about Paul and Barnabas' destiny:

128

"Now there were at Antioch, in the church that was there, prophets and teachers: Barnabas, and Simeon who was called Niger, and Lucius of Cyrene, and Manaen who had been brought up with Herod the tetrarch, and Saul. While they were ministering to the Lord and fasting, the Holy Spirit said, 'Set apart for Me Barnabas and Saul for the work to which I have called them.' Then, when they had fasted and prayed and laid their hands on them, they sent them away." — Acts 13:1–3

They weren't looking to do anything except love the Lord. Then, because of their heart to minister to Him, they received revelation that affected the course of Church history. When I read this passage, I cannot help but think of 2 Chronicles 16:9, which says, *"The eyes of the Lord move to and fro throughout the earth that He may strongly support those whose heart is completely His."* When we set aside time to focus ourselves on God and hear His voice, He notices. It is important to Him. He sees us.

Characteristics of a Wilderness of Revelation

The purpose of the wilderness of revelation is to seek the Lord to know Him more. When we withdraw from others in order to receive revelation about God, we come face to face with His goodness, lovingkindness, and faithfulness. These revelations of His heart restore our souls. Revelation is not simply knowledge about a set of facts—revelation of God is life.[5]

Jesus separated Himself from others so He could hear the voice of His Father and learn His will.[6] In times when my circumstances were difficult, I separated myself from others so I could gain revelation about God's will for my life or a specific situation I was involved in. One of those times occurred during a season when I felt exhausted mentally, physically, and spiritually. It got to the point where all I could do was work in my yard. I picked up sticks and threw them in a fire. As I was doing this, I suddenly heard the Lord speak clearly: "It's okay.

I will pick up sticks with you." When I heard the Lord's voice, I just started to weep.

A few minutes later, my good friend Mitch showed up. He didn't say much. He knew I was struggling, but he also knew that God was doing something. So he just started walking around picking up sticks with Jesus and me. Mitch was the physical manifestation of Jesus for me in that moment. After a while, he came over and prayed for me, and then he left. It was nothing fancy or super spiritual, but it was exactly what I needed, just the right kind of revelation of God and His love. In fact, that was one of the greatest revelations of God's simple love I've ever had.

Strengthen Yourself in the Lord

A wilderness of revelation is a time for us to strengthen our relationship with God. One of the biblical stories that inspires me the most is when David defeated the Amalekites. He was distressed because he had lost his family and everything he possessed. And to top it off, his men wanted to stone him. But David's response was to strengthen himself in the Lord, even before he asked God what he should do (1 Samuel 30:6). To me, that is the main characteristic of the wilderness of revelation—a heart that seeks after the Lord Himself and not just what He can do for us. God is our revelation and provision, and He promises that when we seek Him with all our hearts, we will find Him (Jeremiah 29:13–14). And when we find the Lord, we have everything we need. Again, the main characteristic of the wilderness of revelation is a heart that simply wants the Lord.

A Time and Place of Solitude

We talked about how Jesus would often seek out solitude and quiet places where He could be alone with His Father.[7] We also looked at how a wilderness of revelation isn't solely a special location—it can also be a time. In order for us to receive from

130

the Lord, we sometimes need to go to a specific place, for a period of time, that is set apart from the world's distractions.

One of the most significant moments in Church history was the Day of Pentecost, when the Holy Spirit was poured out on Jesus' followers. My belief is that they were in a wilderness of revelation. They had gone to Jerusalem and were waiting in an upper room until they received what Jesus had promised.[8] I am certain they didn't know what to expect; they were simply praying and seeking the Lord, and when the day came, I bet they were surprised!

Being free from distractions is another characteristic of a wilderness of revelation. We can cease striving, be still, and know that God is God.[9]

Prayer and Fasting

The wilderness of revelation often includes fasting. Remember that one of the main purposes of a wilderness is to seek the Lord with a humble heart.[10] Isaiah wrote that fasting produces humility. When he said not to "hide yourself from your own flesh," he was talking about exposing your needs and not trying to hide your weaknesses. Whenever our needs are exposed, we have the opportunity to walk in humility:

> *"Is it a fast like this which I choose, **a day for a man to humble himself**?*
> *Is it for bowing one's head like a reed*
> *And for spreading out sackcloth and ashes as a bed?*
> *Will you call this a fast, even an acceptable day to the Lord?*
> *Is this not the fast which I choose,*
> *To loosen the bonds of wickedness,*
> *To undo the bands of the yoke,*
> *And to let the oppressed go free*
> *And break every yoke?*
> *Is it not to divide your bread with the hungry*
> *And bring the homeless poor into the house;*
> *When you see the naked, to cover him;*
> *And not to hide yourself from your own flesh?*
> *Then your light will break out like the dawn,*

And your recovery will speedily spring forth;
And your righteousness will go before you;
The glory of the Lord will be your rear guard."
— Isaiah 58:5-8 (emphasis added)

A time of fasting helps us hear the Lord's voice. We see this in Acts 13:1-2, when the church leaders in Antioch heard from God about Paul and Barnabas; God spoke to them when they were "ministering to the Lord and fasting." Quite often in Scripture, God's people entered seasons of fasting in order to receive revelation from Him. There are a number of different types of fasts, from food fasts to entertainment fasts. Sometimes fasting in and of itself can be a wilderness of revelation.When we fast, we are setting aside a thing or activity we potentially have been using as a soulish prop, and anytime we remove the props in our lives, the positive effects of a wilderness can occur.

Meditate on the Treasures of God

Prayer and fasting mean quieting ourselves and setting our minds on "things above" in order to hear and receive from the Lord. There are times, however, when we need to be a little more aggressive in our desire to meet with God, and we do this by engaging our minds and hearts in the practice of meditation.

Meditate in Hebrew means "to moan or mutter." When we meditate on God, we are verbalizing continuously, either with our mouths or in our minds — we are stirring things up. It makes me think of taking a cup of warm water, pouring salt into it, and swirling the liquid around so the salt dissolves. Meditation allows the treasures of God to swirl around in our minds and hearts in such a way that they mix through us completely and become a part of our souls.

Here are a few of the different characteristics of the Lord highlighted by the Psalmists:

"One thing I have asked from the Lord, that I shall seek:
That I may dwell in the house of the Lord all the days of my
life, To behold the beauty of the Lord
And to meditate in His temple." — Psalm 27:4

"I will meditate on all Your work
And muse on Your deeds." — Psalm 77:12

"Make me understand the way of Your precepts,
So I will meditate on Your wonders." — Psalm 119:27

"My eyes anticipate the night watches,
That I may meditate on Your word." — Psalm 119:148

"I remember the days of old;
I meditate on all Your doings;
I muse on the work of Your hands." — Psalm 143:5

We have such a treasure in God. He is like a vast chest of riches, and He longs to impart all of Himself to our souls. As we meditate on Him and His greatness, the process saturates us with the waters of Heaven; it refreshes and changes our souls. By meditating on God in a wilderness of revelation, we set the tone and direction of our hearts and minds.

Search Out the Treasures of God's Word

In the wilderness of revelation, another "aggressive" way to set the direction of our souls is by studying God's Word. Examining the Bible — really searching it out for hidden treasures — was considered a characteristic of greatness in Ezra and the saints in Thessalonica:

"For Ezra had set his heart to study the law of the Lord and to practice it, and to teach His statutes and ordinances in Israel." — Ezra 7:10

"Now these were more noble-minded than those in Thessalonica, for they received the word with great eagerness, examining the Scriptures daily to see whether these things were so." — Acts 17:11

When I search the Bible, I feel like I am wading through a beautiful mountain stream and panning for gold. God's Word is great, and the Holy Spirit is so very willing to reveal the deep things of God that are written in its pages.[11] When we are in a wilderness of revelation, it is very important to spend time in the Word and allow the Holy Spirit to reveal treasures and truths contained within it.

Reasons for the Wilderness of Revelation

The wilderness of revelation is not a time of punishment or forced discipline; it is a time to set ourselves apart for the Lord. It is a time to enjoy Him. We seek God for the sake of God Himself, not for what we can receive from Him, because when we have Him, we have what we need. He knows what we need even before we ask.[12]

When I am pursuing my wife just for what I can get out of our relationship, I can easily make her feel used. But when my heart is to be with Paula just because I love her, it brings things into balance. In the same way, when we set our hearts to seek God—believing that when we have Him, we will receive what we need—it brings things into balance. Seeking after God for who He is enables us to receive Him as the good God He is.[13]

He is Jehovah. When we have Him, we have Jehovah-Jireh, our Provider; Jehovah-Rapha, our Healer, and Jehovah-Shalom, our Peace. We have El Shaddai, the One who is more than enough for us. Obviously, there are times when we need to ask Him for His provision and help, but the foundation of a wilderness of revelation is a heart that is after God alone, not what He can do for us.

Saturate Yourself in God's Presence

God's presence is the main purpose of a wilderness of revelation. He is always with us, and our bodies are temples of His

Holy Spirit, yet there are times when we purposefully need to allow the Lord to fill us with His reality. Exiled to the island of Patmos, John took an opportunity to saturate himself in the Spirit of God, and the result was the Book of Revelation, a massive prophecy. He wrote, *"I was in the Spirit on the Lord's day, and I heard behind me a loud voice like the sound of a trumpet"* (Revelation 1:10).

Likewise, when David was in the wilderness of Judah, his main passion was to seek God's presence:

> *"O God, You are my God; I shall seek You earnestly;*
> *My soul thirsts for You, my flesh yearns for You,*
> *In a dry and weary land where there is no water.*
> *Thus I have seen You in the sanctuary,*
> *To see Your power and Your glory.*
> *Because Your lovingkindness is better than life,*
> *My lips will praise You."*   — Psalm 63:1–3

Even when those who hated him were threatening his life, David sought the presence of the Lord:

> *"Hear, O Lord, when I cry with my voice,*
> *And be gracious to me and answer me.*
> *When You said, 'Seek My face [presence],' my heart said to*
> *You, 'Your face [presence], O Lord, I shall seek.'"*
>   — Psalm 27:7–8

David constantly sought the presence of God, and then while resting in God's presence, he would inquire about the needs he had and the perilous situations he found himself in. When he sought God and God alone, not His provision or protection, David was filled with God's fullness and goodness. As I said, it isn't wrong to seek God for the things we need, but I am emphasizing here that our first priority in a wilderness of revelation is the Lord Himself, and our inquiries come second.

In our church we have about six conferences, retreats, or "encounters" (specialized retreats focused on meeting with the Lord and experiencing His presence) every year. These events work well for a wilderness of revelation because people have the opportunity to separate themselves from distractions and concentrate on one major goal: gaining revelation of God.

One time I took a group of interns away for a weekend simply to seek the Lord. On Saturday night as we worshipped together, several things happened. I looked up and in my mind's eye saw Jesus standing behind one of the young men. It was a very strong impression. Another young man, lying facedown on the floor worshipping, saw a robed figure step over him, and my good friend Leigha kept hearing the same word repeated in an unknown spiritual language. Later as we were talking, we realized all of it had happened at the same time. Leigha told us the word she'd been hearing, and I recognized it as Hebrew. I looked it up in a Hebrew dictionary, and to our amazement, it meant "he is here." I realized that I really did see the Lord, and it wasn't just my imagination. The things the Lord revealed to me out of that experience still affect my words and actions today.

The express purpose of a wilderness of revelation is to seek the Lord Himself. When you withdraw from the world to go meet with God, He will make certain you are successful.

Gain Revelation of God

If Jesus put Himself in a wilderness of revelation to hear from His Father, it makes sense that we should do the same.

When we choose to enter a wilderness of revelation, we are removing the support and comfort of the flesh and soul. Subconsciously, we depend on so many things other than the Lord to meet our nine soulish needs: love, identity, acceptance, worth, intimacy, security, purpose, forgiveness, and the need to be needed.[A] One of the main ways our soulish needs are met is with God's Word.[14] When we try to meet our soulish needs through other people, work, hobbies, and so forth, we sedate ourselves from receiving God's Word.

It is like giving donuts to people who are starving. Yes, the donuts will sedate their hunger, but it will not satisfy their physical nutritional needs. If they continued to eat donuts and didn't eat anything else, eventually they would get sick and could even die of malnutrition. It is the same for us in the spiritual realm. We were created to feed on the spiritual words of God. His Word nourishes our entire being.[15]

When we depend on anything other than Jesus, we are sedating our souls and dulling our spiritual senses. Strong painkillers numb the mind's ability to feel and think. When we sedate our soulish needs with human resources, we dull the spirit's ability to feel and receive revelation. In a wilderness of revelation, we are attempting to reposition ourselves to receive spiritual revelation from a spiritual God.[11] God is a spiritual being, and in order to receive and hear from Him, we need to tune in to the spiritual realm, specifically the Holy Spirit. Sometimes we take a wrong approach in trying to hear from God; we try to listen to Him intellectually or with our souls. The problem with this kind of effort is that it doesn't allow us to discern anything from the Spirit. *"But a natural [soulish] man does not accept the things of the Spirit of God, for they are foolishness to him; and he cannot understand them, because they are spiritually appraised"* (1 Corinthians 2:14). We need to come to God in the "frequency" of the spirit. Gaining revelation soulishly is like trying to listen to a radio station without a radio. To listen to radio waves, we need a radio!

Another common distraction is the flesh. Paul wrote in 1 Corinthians 3:1–5 that the fleshly mind cannot handle spiritual revelation. It is focused on the state of the physical or fleshly realm. Am I tired? Am I hungry? Am I successful? Am I prosperous? Am I resting in my worldly accomplishments and recognitions? As we enter a wilderness of revelation, we are setting aside our fleshly and worldly recognitions, accomplishments, and confidences and allowing the "spirit man" to rule. We are choosing to shut off certain physical needs (through fasting) in order to quiet the distracting voices of the flesh and soul and, therefore, hear God more clearly.

Break the Bonds of Enslavement

Time spent in the wilderness of revelation breaks our bonds. That is an important benefit. We know that Jesus came to earth to set us free,[16] and a wilderness of revelation is one of those places where the freedom of the Lord can be received.

David wrote, *"Let my judgment come forth from Your presence"* (Psalm 17:2). In God's presence, we can see, hear, and feel clearly what is keeping us (or the people we are ministering to) in bondage. We can discern whether the enslavement is a lack of knowledge, a flesh pattern, a stronghold, or some other type of bondage. Let me explain what I mean.

It is unfortunate how a seemingly "simple" lack of knowledge can be so enslaving. Isaiah 5:13 tells us that God's people are taken into exile or captivity through a lack of knowledge. I remember a clear example of this that startled the ministry team and me. One night, a woman with a smoking addiction (a type of enslavement) came to us for prayer. She wanted to break this addiction in her life but had been unable to do so. We began the prayer time by worshipping the Lord, playing a song by Phil Driscoll about the holiness of God. As the song ended, I looked up, and the woman was walking down the aisle to exit the sanctuary.

"Where are you going?" I called after her.

"I am free!" she replied.

"What do you mean you are free?"

In confidence, she said something that still imprints my heart to this day: "He is holy. I am holy. I am free!" She turned and walked out of the sanctuary, and to the best of my knowledge, she has never smoked again. In a wilderness of revelation, we can discover the truth of God that sets us free.

A flesh pattern is a pattern of lustful thoughts that seeks to dominate a person's ability to choose. Peter wrote, *"Beloved, I urge you as aliens and strangers to abstain from fleshly lusts which wage war against the soul"* (1 Peter 2:11). The Greek word for "lust" can literally mean "upon the mind with force." In other words, our flesh shoots forceful thoughts into the soul, trying to dominate the soul's choices. The flesh wants to be preeminent and cause the soul to adopt a fleshly identity. In a wilderness of revelation, we separate ourselves from the temptations of fleshly lust in order to set our minds on living to the spirit. In this way, we allow our souls (the heart and mind) to break off the flesh's dominance[17] and set ourselves in a new direction — that of living to Jesus.

Another type of bondage is a stronghold. I define a stronghold as anything that blocks us off from God's presence, provisions, or truth. Paul wrote in 2 Corinthians 10:3–6 that when we destroy strongholds, we are making our obedience to the Lord complete; then when our obedience is complete, we are able to punish every disobedience (that is, we can remove the spiritual strongholds the enemy would potentially use to hinder us). In the wilderness of revelation, God's glory can be revealed in our hearts — that is, we begin to see Him in greater detail. Glory often means thoughts, opinions, and recognition, and when we speak of the glory of God, we mean the revelation of who God is. Yet the glory of God can also denote His thoughts and opinions of us — who we are. So when we see the glory of God clearly, and are able to receive that glory into our minds and hearts, we are empowered to lay aside the strongholds that are enslaving us.[18B]

Spiritual enslavement occurs when a person has allowed a stronghold to be demonically enhanced by repetitively or intensely giving in to the stronghold.

> *"The Lord's bond-servant must not be quarrelsome, but be kind to all, able to teach, patient when wronged, with gentleness correcting those who are in opposition, if perhaps God may grant them repentance leading to the knowledge of the truth, and they may come to their senses and escape from the snare of the devil, having been held captive by him to do his will."* — 2 Timothy 2:24–26

Our Father's heart is to see us set free from demonic enslavements. A wilderness of revelation is a good time for perceiving the root issues that are holding us captive, and once they are revealed, we can deal with them. When we know the root of the enslavement, we can take care of the problem.

I am aware that demonic torment, or what I often call enslavement, is a controversial subject. However, after three decades of ministry, I strongly believe demonic spirits can torment and even enslave both non-believers and believers. The Bible verifies it is possible for a Christian to be impacted by the demonic realm.[19] I have seen thousands of people set free from various forms of demonic enslavements, and I am continually amazed at the number of different emotions a demonic spirit can generate in a person: fears, pains, anxieties, paralyses, different types of anger and confusion, and so forth. When we enter God's presence during a time of wilderness, it helps put all of these things in perspective.

When Jesus came off the Mount of Transfiguration, which was an incredible spiritual encounter, He found His disciples trying to cast a strong demonic spirit out of a young boy. When they weren't successful, they asked Jesus why they couldn't do it. Part of His answer was Matthew 17:21: *"This kind does not go out except by prayer and fasting."* He was able to drive the demon out because He had been with His Father. When we separate ourselves in a wilderness of revelation, we are able to soak in God's presence, and the chains of the enemy fall away from our souls.

The wilderness of revelation positions us to see, hear, and feel the truth of God more clearly, and God's truth always sets us free. A few years ago, a friend of mine wanted to set himself apart to the Lord and remove anything that hindered his relationship with Him. He went into a season of prayer and fasting, and one night when he was home with his wife, he manifested a demonic spirit of anger. Anger rose up in him, and he put his fist through a wall.

His wife gently took him by the face, looked him in the eyes, and said, "I do not know who or what you are, but in the name of Jesus Christ, get out of here!" Her husband dropped into a comatose-like state. She led him over to the bed, and he slept most of the next day until our senior and associate pastors went over to help. As they were praying for him, the Lord revealed that when he was in the Vietnam conflict, he had used anger to protect himself. Later he had continued to use anger in his business dealings; he thought it helped him get things done. Ephesians 4:26–27 tells us not to let the sun go down on our anger, or we will give the devil a place in our lives. He had given the devil a place, but he was set free as he focused on the Lord in a wilderness of revelation.

We never have to talk the Lord into coming to us. Isaiah 30:18 says that He waits on high to have compassion on us and wants to be gracious to us. He longs to come and love us. He looks for us, as 2 Chronicles 16:9 says: *"For the eyes of the Lord move to and fro throughout the earth that He may strongly support those whose heart is completely His."* A wilderness of revelation is an opportunity for our hearts to come in line with God's heart — and His heart is to meet with us.

God has given His whole heart for us, and with that whole heart, He seeks us out. In our human frailty, our hearts do not always want to meet with God, but we have a promise that when we seek the Lord, we will find Him.[20] It is like two lovers finally reuniting after being apart for a long time. In a wilderness of revelation, we have the opportunity to allow our hearts to long for the One whose heart is after us.

God in the Wilderness

The enemy designed the pressures of this world to draw the life of God out of our souls. Knowing this, one of my favorite things to do is walk in the woods by myself and pray and meditate on the Lord. Each of these times, however brief, is a wilderness of revelation, and my soul is refreshed and strengthened with the Lord's beauty and goodness.

A wilderness of revelation is a time or season we choose to enter for different reasons. A common reason is to seek refreshing from the Lord. Sometimes we need to withdraw from the pressures and drains of life in order to hear Him better. At other times, it is not so much the drain of life as it is the desire to get away from distractions, just so we can receive new revelation from Him.

Another reason for a wilderness of revelation is that our hearts are wounded and broken from trauma, and we need God's loving and restoring presence to saturate and heal our souls. We also can enter a wilderness of revelation simply because we long to love the Lord and let Him express His love to us. Whatever the reason we choose to enter this wilderness, it is a time to pursue an unveiling of God and His awesome attributes.

A wilderness of revelation is different than any other type of wilderness. For example, both the wilderness of sin and death and the wilderness of transition are seasons imposed on us by life circumstances or the Lord's leadership. A wilderness of revelation, however, is a conscious choice on our part to saturate ourselves in God's presence, receive revelation from Him, or break the bonds of enslavement. We find a time and place of solitude, strengthen ourselves in the Lord, pray and fast, meditate on God's goodness, and study His Word.

Whatever reason we have for employing the wilderness of revelation, we deepen our relationship with God every time we choose to withdraw from the world to focus on Him.

Notes / Reference Scriptures

A. To learn more about our physical, soulish and spiritual needs, I recomment my book entitled - *Jesus: The Filler of Needs*.

B. To learn more about strongholds and other types of spiritual bondage, please refer to my book - *Breaking Free of Strongholds*. For more information visit dealingjesus.org

1. John 5:19
2. Psalm 25:12
3. Matthew 14:22-23
4. Psalm 23:3
5. John 17:3
6. Luke 6:12, 22:39-42
7. Luke 5:15-16, 6:12-13
8. Acts 1:13-14

9. Psalm 46:10
10. Deuteronomy 8:2-3

11. 1 Corinthians 2:9-10
12. Matthew 6:8
13. 1 Timothy 6:17
14. Matthew 4:1-4
15. Proverbs 4:20-22
16. Galatians 5:13
17. Romans 6:11-12
18. 2 Corinthians 3:18;
    Hebrews 12:1-2
19. Acts 5:3; 2 Timothy 2:26
20. Jeremiah 29:13

8 The Self-Imposed Wilderness

Most of the time, we enter the wilderness of revelation on purpose. We put ourselves into that wilderness because we want to hear God's voice and reconnect with Him.

A self-imposed wilderness is similar in that we put ourselves into it on purpose; however, it occurs when we are running from God in some form or another, not running to Him. It is not the wilderness of sin and death, which is caused by blatant disobedience, but it arises when we are consciously or subconsciously trying to escape from life, responsibility, relationships, and many times even God.

I am unfortunately familiar with the self-imposed wilderness. I have turned tail and run into this wilderness a number of times. A few years ago, I was completely overwhelmed by life. With my dad, I was involved in running our real estate holding company in Florida. I was also involved with a massive business deal in which we were negotiating to sell our company; included in that was a huge gas spill at one of our rental locations that had to be cleaned up, the cost of which came to about one million dollars. Paula and I had purchased land in Virginia for the development of a retreat center. I was helping develop a sub-division on one part of the property, as well as working to put a conservation easement on another part of the property. At one point, I counted and realized that I was involved in hiring six different law firms to navigate us through all the things we had going on.

At the same time, I was the senior elder and pastor in Dwelling Place Christian Fellowship and heading up the church's internship program. I was traveling overseas and ministering in the Middle East, Sweden, Greece, Serbia, and Macedonia. I was trying to be a husband to Paula and a dad to Shea and Michele. Needless to say, I was a little overwhelmed.

At the end of my rope, in my heart I ended up withdrawing from leading in the church. I might not have physically separated myself, but mentally and spiritually, I withdrew into a self-imposed wilderness. I shut my heart and emotions down in an effort to survive.

We can experience a self-imposed wilderness when we are broken, rejected, wounded, tired, overwhelmed, depressed, hopeless, confused, or feeling guilty. In any of these conditions, we tend to run and hide. Desperate, we separate ourselves from God and other people, and the self-imposed wilderness comes about as we take things into our own hands. This wilderness is the fruit of our own efforts.

Examples of a Self-Imposed Wilderness

The self-imposed wilderness is one of pain and sorrow. To find everyday examples of people who are going through this wilderness, all we have to do is look for those who are hurting and tired. Let's look at three examples of this wilderness found in Scripture.

Elijah's Trial

> "Then Jezebel sent a messenger to Elijah, saying, 'So may the gods do to me and even more, if I do not make your life as the life of one of them by tomorrow about this time.' And he was afraid and arose and ran for his life and came to Beersheba, which belongs to Judah, and left his servant there. But he himself went a day's journey into the wil-

derness, and came and sat down under a juniper tree; and he requested for himself that he might die, and said, 'It is enough; now, O Lord, take my life, for I am not better than my fathers.'" — 1 Kings 19:2–4

Elijah had just confronted the prophets of Baal, which no doubt mentally drained him. He was dealing with physical weariness, having run the first "marathon" from the top of Mount Carmel to Jezreel (approximately twenty-five miles). Likely, he could also sense the intense spiritual warfare surrounding the demonic spirit that enslaved Jezebel and both influenced and enhanced her actions. We know this type of spiritual environment exists because Jesus addressed it in His message to the church at Thyatira.[1] The spiritual pressure Elijah faced was very real and intimidating. He had it rough.

Scripture implies that the weariness of ministry, all the warfare, and Elijah's wild journey into the desert to escape Jezebel were more than he could handle. He retreated into a self-imposed wilderness, wanting God to end it all and put him out of his misery. God met him there and called him out of his pity party, commissioning him to finish his course and thereby setting in motion the generation of the prophetic ministry that was to follow.

Moses and His Destiny

Before Moses delivered Israel out of Egypt, he experienced a wilderness. He started off with zeal, trying to fulfill the destiny that burned in his heart—that of bringing the Hebrews out of Egypt.[2] But the ones he believed he was supposed to help ended up rejecting him,[3] and it becomes clear that disillusionment set into his heart:

"At this remark, Moses fled and became an alien in the land of Midian, where he became the father of two sons. After forty years had passed, an angel appeared to him in the wilderness of Mount Sinai, in the flame of a burning thorn bush. When Moses saw it, he marveled at the sight; and as

145

he approached to look more closely, there came the voice of the Lord . . . This Moses whom they disowned, saying, 'Who made you a ruler and a judge?' is the one whom God sent to be both a ruler and a deliverer with the help of the angel who appeared to him in the thorn bush."   — Acts 7:29–35

Moses was disenchanted with life. His discouragement was so great that he even forgot how he used to operate. It is interesting that in Acts 7:22, while still a young man in Egypt, Moses was described as a "man of power in words and deeds," but when the Lord appeared to him in the wilderness, Moses had trouble speaking, and he was not confident in his ability to carry out the task the Lord had for him. He told God, *"Please, Lord, I have never been eloquent, neither recently nor in time past, nor since You have spoken to Your servant; for I am slow of speech and slow of tongue"* (Exodus 4:10).

It is common in a self-imposed wilderness for a person to entertain lies about his or her abilities. But God caused good to come out of Moses' situation by infusing his character with humility: *"Now the man Moses was very humble, more than any man who was on the face of the earth"* (Numbers 12:3). This humility was the result of God's love and His work within Moses.

Jonah's Confusion

A self-imposed wilderness can also be caused by running from the call of God on our lives. In the first chapter of Jonah, God told him to go to Nineveh and cry against the city, but Jonah fled.[4] He entered a self-imposed wilderness when he tried to escape God's call and subsequently had the famous encounter with the fish.[5]

After Jonah preached in Nineveh, he entered a second self-imposed wilderness. He became angry when he saw that God was going to spare the city instead of destroying it:

"But it greatly displeased Jonah and he became angry. He prayed to the Lord and said, 'Please Lord, was not this what

I said while I was still in my own country? Therefore in order to forestall this I fled to Tarshish, for I knew that You are a gracious and compassionate God, slow to anger and abundant in lovingkindness, and one who relents concerning calamity. Therefore now, O Lord, please take my life from me, for death is better to me than life.'"
— Jonah 4:1–3

In both of these instances, Jonah was disillusioned and confused by God's mercy toward the ruthless Assyrians, and he made his situation worse when he tried to take matters into his own hands.

These examples show us the humanity of the heroes of Scripture. There were times when they fell into the trap of thinking or feeling that what they faced was more than they could handle. But God sought to redeem them out of their despair.

Characteristics of a Self-Imposed Wilderness

As with every type of wilderness, it is important for us to discern what is going on in our lives. When we recognize that we are in a self-imposed wilderness, we can respond appropriately and allow the Lord to bring good out of a season of pain.

The following are some of the characteristics of a self-imposed wilderness. Keep in mind that not all of these occur when a person goes through this type of wilderness; he or she could experience only one or two of these characteristics.

Emotional Intensity

Immediately after we have gone through an intense season, it is normal for our pendulum of emotional energy to swing in the opposite direction. In 1 Kings 18, Elijah confronted the prophets of Baal and outran the king's chariot. He saw a tremendous, miraculous victory. But when he received a death threat from

Jezebel, his emotions suddenly swung from victory to defeat. In Moses' story in Exodus, his self-imposed wilderness was more long term. He suffered from the rejection of his people and the threat of Pharaoh. After the resurrection, Peter put himself into a self-imposed wilderness when he went back to fishing. He had endured the emotional pain of denying Jesus, and then he faced the massive trauma of watching someone he loved be humiliated and hung on a cross. Each of these intense emotional times led to a self-imposed wilderness of some kind.

As a modern-day example, pastors often experience depression and a form of hopelessness on Monday mornings due to the weight of their Sunday responsibilities. These emotions come from a variety of sources. Very often, pastors stay up late finishing the sermon and then wake up early the next morning to get to church. They can be weighed down by the spiritual potency of a worship service and by seeing the pain of people they care about. They can start wondering what the congregation thought of the sermon, and they commonly carry the spiritual emotions that come as believers pray for one another. All of these emotional and physical issues can weigh on a person's soul and push him or her into the self-imposed wilderness on Monday morning.

Thoughts of Defeat and Hopelessness

Thoughts of defeat and hopelessness are two of the most pronounced characteristics of a self-imposed wilderness. This type of thinking actually compels us into the wilderness in the first place. Again using pastors as an example, they can easily entertain feelings and thoughts of hopelessness and defeat when they have tried to do their best, but someone criticizes the way they spoke or the content of what they said.

Elijah clearly felt defeated in 1 Kings 19. He told God, *"It is enough; now, O Lord, take my life, for I am not better than my fathers"* (verse 4). Jonah said something similar: *"Therefore now, O Lord, please take my life from me, for death is better to me than life"* (Jonah 4:3).

The prophet Jeremiah watched as an enemy defeated his country and his people were sold as slaves. As he dealt with a self-imposed wilderness, he expressed the hopelessness in his heart:

> *"My soul has been rejected from peace;*
> *I have forgotten happiness.*
> *So I say, 'My strength has perished,*
> *And so has my hope from the Lord.'*
> *Remember my affliction and my wandering, the wormwood*
> *and bitterness.*
> *Surely my soul remembers*
> *And is bowed down within me."*
>
> — Lamentations 3:17–20

The intensity of the feelings can vary, but these thoughts of defeat and hopelessness are a common characteristic of the self-imposed wilderness.

Physical and Emotional Weariness

Physical weariness is another characteristic of the self-imposed wilderness. After Elijah poured out his heart to God and declared how hopeless he was, he fell asleep. Sleep can be a symptom of depression, and in this instance, it seems that Elijah's physical weariness helped create the environment for his depression and hopelessness.

We can also become emotionally weary in a self-imposed wilderness. Jeremiah's confession in Lamentations 3:17–20 shows how emotionally weary he was: *"I have forgotten happiness. So I say, 'My strength has perished.'"* The joy of the Lord is our strength, and when our circumstances distract our focus from Him, we lose our emotional and subsequently physical strength.

> *"Then God said to Jonah, 'Do you have good reason to be*
> *angry about the plant?' And he said, 'I have good reason to*
> *be angry, even to death.'"* — Jonah 4:9

149

God's Response in the Self-Imposed Wilderness

The self-imposed wilderness is not God-initiated, yet He still works with us to cause good things to come out of this season. God loves us sincerely and does not abandon us in these times; always He seeks to draw us to Himself. Here are some of God's responses when one of His children enters a self-imposed wilderness.

God Shows Mercy and Compassion

God is patient with us so we can be healed, strengthened, restored, and released into the purposes He has for us. Isaiah 42:2–3 describes God's heart for the person who has run into a self-imposed wilderness:

> *"He will not cry out or raise His voice,*
> *Nor make His voice heard in the street.*
> *A bruised reed He will not break*
> *And a dimly burning wick He will not extinguish;*
> *He will faithfully bring forth justice."*

This passage reflects the tenderness of God toward the broken, wounded, tired, depressed, hopeless, and confused. There aren't many things more tender or vulnerable than a "bruised" reed or a dimly burning wick. The slightest act of aggression would destroy the reed and extinguish the light. God will be gentle with us, and He will comfort the broken hearted and poor in spirit.[6]

Most of the time, people in a self-imposed wilderness are barely able to function spiritually. They feel confused and often guilt ridden, as if they're letting God down, when God looks at them with love, mercy, grace, and compassion. Even when Jonah was angry and disillusioned, the Lord was merciful and compassionate toward him.

150

Whenever I encounter a self-imposed wilderness, the Lord is so gracious to my wounded and tired heart. We have an awesome God who is full of mercy and gentleness, even when we are weary and running from Him.

God Comforts and Strengthens

In His love and compassion, God works to comfort, strengthen, and commission those who are in a self-imposed wilderness. When Elijah was in the wilderness, the Lord expressed His compassion toward him by taking care of him. He provided food and a place to rest:

> *"He lay down and slept under a juniper tree; and behold, there was an angel touching him, and he said to him, 'Arise, eat.' Then he looked and behold, there was at his head a bread cake baked on hot stones, and a jar of water. So he ate and drank and lay down again. The angel of the Lord came again a second time and touched him and said, 'Arise, eat, because the journey is too great for you.' So he arose and ate and drank, and went in the strength of that food forty days and forty nights to Horeb, the mountain of God."*
> — 1 Kings 19:5–8

When Jonah was full of anger and self-pity, God gave him a tree to protect him from the heat:

> *"'Therefore now, O Lord, please take my life from me, for death is better to me than life.' The Lord said, 'Do you have good reason to be angry?' Then Jonah went out from the city and sat east of it. There he made a shelter for himself and sat under it in the shade until he could see what would happen in the city. So the Lord God appointed a plant and it grew up over Jonah to be a shade over his head to deliver him from his discomfort. And Jonah was extremely happy about the plant."*
> — Jonah 4:3–6

The tree was an expression of the lovingkindness of God for a man who was confused and disillusioned. (We will talk more about the tree in a moment.) For the person who has entered a self-imposed wilderness, the only thing that can help is the Lord's heart to heal and restore. He will strengthen those who are tired and wounded.

God Deals with Strongholds

When we are in a self-imposed wilderness, our heavenly Father works to reveal and remove any thinking that would hinder true, complete comfort and strengthening.

When my kids were young, it was a semi-traumatic experience whenever they got a splinter. They acted like I was killing them as I tried to get the splinter out. But I was trying to help them. I was pulling the splinter from the hand or foot because I loved my child. If I left the splinter, it could have caused problems later on—I was removing what needed to be removed so the healing process could take place. In a similar fashion, God works to remove the "splinters" of life that have permeated our hearts so true comfort, healing, and strength can come to us.

Sometimes in the short run, true comfort does not seem like comfort at all. In Jonah's story, it was God's lovingkindness to allow a tree to grow up and provide comfort for the weary, confused prophet. But then God almost seems cruel as, the very next day, He "commissioned" a worm to destroy the tree. He gave comfort and then removed comfort.

Yet this serves only to tell us that God's lovingkindness for Jonah extended to his soul. God was working to remove the anger, hatred, and injustice in Jonah's heart toward a people who had no knowledge of God:

> *"But God appointed a worm when dawn came the next day and it attacked the plant and it withered. When the sun came up God appointed a scorching east wind, and the sun beat down on Jonah's head so that he became faint and begged with all his soul to die, saying, 'Death is better to me than life.' Then God said to Jonah, 'Do you have good reason to be angry about the plant?' And he said, 'I have good reason to be angry, even to death.' Then the Lord said, 'You had compassion on the plant for which you did not work and which you did not cause to grow, which came up over-*

night and perished overnight. Should I not have compassion on Nineveh, the great city in which there are more than 120,000 persons who do not know the difference between their right and left hand, as well as many animals?'"

— Jonah 4:7–11

God was being merciful. If the tree had continued to live, it would have simply covered up the anger, death, unrighteousness, and lack of mercy filling Jonah's heart. God was trying to help Jonah let go of things that were hurting him.

In the midst of comforting Elijah, God was working to reveal lies that were hurting Elijah's soul. Elijah believed that he was alone, when there were seven thousand who had not bowed to Baal.[7] Elijah was entertaining some bitterness toward his own people; he was touting his own righteousness, declaring that he had been zealous for the Lord, while Israel had committed murder and was unrighteous. God actually loved and comforted Elijah by allowing him to process the loneliness, pain, and weariness that were churning in his soul.

Being weary and feeling pain aren't the recipe for a wilderness of sin and death — they won't automatically land a person in that type of wilderness — but they do cause the soul to feel weighed down and heavy, and we are in need of the Lord's comfort.

God Directs and Commissions

Once the Lord has comforted and strengthened the person caught in a self-imposed wilderness, He works to direct and commission that person out of the wilderness.

After Jesus died on the cross, the disciples fell into fear and defeat:

"Simon Peter, and Thomas called Didymus, and Nathanael of Cana in Galilee, and the sons of Zebedee, and two others of His disciples were together. Simon Peter said to them, 'I am going fishing.' They said to him, 'We will also come with you.' They went out and got into the boat; and that night they caught nothing." — John 21:2–3

In this passage, we see a defeated Peter going back to his past occupation of fishing. He was running away, filled with the guilt of his denial and his fears of the future. Jesus came to the disciples and gave them instructions, essentially telling them how to be successful in what Peter wanted to do — catch a large number of fish. But here is the interesting thing: As they were bringing in their catch, Peter jumped into the water. At first, it seems that he jumped out of the boat in order to go meet Jesus, but a second read reveals that Peter was actually hiding. He wasn't trying to reach Jesus first. He was trying to reach Him last:

> *"Therefore that disciple whom Jesus loved said to Peter, 'It is the Lord.' So when Simon Peter heard that it was the Lord, he put his outer garment on (for he was stripped for work), and threw himself into the sea. But the other disciples came in the little boat, for they were not far from the land, but about one hundred yards away, dragging the net full of fish. So when they got out on the land, they saw a charcoal fire already laid and fish placed on it, and bread. Jesus said to them, 'Bring some of the fish which you have now caught.' Simon Peter went up and drew the net to land, full of large fish, a hundred and fifty-three; and although there were so many, the net was not torn."*   — John 21:7–11

Peter was the last man to come up out of the water. He wasn't eager; he was afraid. His heart hurt because of his sin. He had run headfirst into a self-imposed wilderness.

During their time on the shore, the Lord said nothing negative to Peter. Instead, He began the process of redeeming Peter's broken heart. As I wrote earlier, the sense of smell is one of the greatest imprinters of information on the human heart. Around a charcoal fire, Peter had denied Jesus three times.[8] After His resurrection, Jesus cooked breakfast over the same type of fire, with the same smell, and He commissioned Peter three times. In other words, in the midst of Peter's self-imposed wilderness, Jesus came and found him in order to spend time with him, comfort him, and commission him into his destiny.

Elijah had a similar experience with the Lord during his self-imposed wilderness. The Lord repeatedly asked him, "What are you doing here?" Each time, Elijah responded in defeat and self-pity:

"Then he came there to a cave and lodged there; and behold, the word of the Lord came to him, and He said to him, 'What are you doing here, Elijah?' He said, 'I have been very zealous for the Lord, the God of hosts; for the sons of Israel have forsaken Your covenant, torn down Your altars and killed Your prophets with the sword. And I alone am left; and they seek my life, to take it away.'" — 1 Kings 19:9–10

The Lord was merciful and compassionate toward Elijah and did not allow him to stay in the wilderness. Instead, He gave Elijah responsibilities:

"The Lord said to him, 'Go, return on your way to the wilderness of Damascus, and when you have arrived, you shall anoint Hazael king over Aram; and Jehu the son of Nimshi you shall anoint king over Israel; and Elisha the son of Shaphat of Abel-meholah you shall anoint as prophet in your place.'" — 1 Kings 19:15–16

After commissioning Elisha, his successor, Elijah had an experience like no other person in the whole of Scripture. He was taken into Heaven in a fiery chariot. Clearly, God was not disappointed with His child.

When we are in a self-imposed wilderness—tired from life's burdens, depressed, or running from what God is asking us to do—He wants to comfort, strengthen, and heal us. He also wants to call us out of the wilderness by commissioning us afresh with His will and purpose.

Responding to God in a Self-Imposed Wilderness

If you have found yourself in a self-imposed wilderness, the following steps could help you overcome the circumstances that led you there. The key is to refocus yourself on the reality of God.

Allow Yourself to Rest

When we are facing tough circumstances, sometimes the most spiritual thing we can do is rest. Tiredness and depression can easily distort our perspective of the past, present, and future. When Elijah went into the wilderness, the Lord directed him to rest.[9] When Jesus learned that His cousin John had died, He encouraged the disciples to come away with Him to a secluded place to rest.[10] Resting helps create an environment in which we can clearly hear the Lord and gain insight into His truth concerning our lives and the future. When I am in a self-imposed wilderness, rest helps set me straight.

We need to rest before we make any major decision. I have made a few decisions in the wilderness — in the midst of depression and discouragement, when I could not hear God clearly — and those decisions ended up causing pain. Rest is an important factor in overcoming a self-imposed wilderness.

Be Refreshed

In the self-imposed wilderness, we need to be refreshed, and the Lord wants us to be refreshed.

When Elijah was in the wilderness, twice an angel of the Lord came to him and gave him food and drink.[11] The Lord wanted to prepare Elijah physically for the journey he was about to take.

It is important to note that the Lord was not asking Elijah to fast during this time, even though most of us consider fasting "more spiritual" than taking care of ourselves. The Lord wanted Elijah to rest and be refreshed. In a self-imposed wilderness, fasting is not necessarily a good activity. It isn't a time for sacrifice and additional strain but a time to allow the Lord to bring refreshment.

It is easy to fall into a rut of helplessness, hopelessness, and self-abasement. Both Elijah and Jonah entertained thoughts of death. They just wanted to die. But when we allow the Lord's rest and refreshment to come into our souls, He puts us in an environment that breaks the mindset of heaviness. In a self-imposed wilderness, we can't focus on what is wrong with us or what we need to sacrifice in our lives—it is a time to focus on God's nature and heart for us.

Dwell on the Character of God

It is very common to look for a quick way out in the self-imposed wilderness, an escape, but this wilderness is a time to rest and be reestablished in God's character.

For Jonah, the self-imposed wilderness was a journey of discovering the depths of God's lovingkindness and compassion. For Elijah, the self-imposed wilderness was a time to rediscover the Lord's faithfulness and wisdom. He saw that the purpose of God was good and the Lord had been, and still was, working to bring about that good purpose.

For Moses, the self-imposed wilderness was a time to discover who Yahweh God really was. Peter discovered Jesus' compassion and love. Jeremiah mourned in his hopelessness and despair, but when he started declaring the character of God, hope returned to his heart.

When we realize we are in a self-imposed wilderness, we need to look for what God is doing. What is He trying to tell us? The Holy Spirit is giving us revelation about God's nature, and we need to allow our hearts to receive it.

Sometimes a key to allowing our hearts to hear the Lord is quieting and stilling ourselves from life's activities so we can just listen. Psalm 46:10 says, *"Be still, and know that I am God"* (NKJV). At other times, we simply need to be willing to hear what the Lord is saying, because we have closed our hearts to what He wants to say. Whenever this happens, it means we have received a lie about God; we have started to think that He is not going to give us what is best for our lives. But God is always good, and our souls are designed to rest in the revelation of His goodness.

Once when I was in this wilderness, I knew I needed to saturate myself in God's lovingkindness and faithfulness. To receive as much revelation on the topic as I could, I printed out a list of every verse in Scripture that used those two words. Every morning, I focused on a verse about God's lovingkindness, and every night before I went to sleep, I focused on verses that spoke of God's faithfulness. I allowed the revelation of His lovingkindness and faithfulness to fill my heart and mind.

Another time, in another wilderness, I thought I was a failure, and the Holy Spirit highlighted God's justice and righteousness to me. The grace and mercy of God became my focus. In the self-imposed wilderness, the Holy Spirit is so faithful to direct our hearts toward God's truth. On the foundation of God's nature and character — that is, through the truth He is speaking to us right now — the Lord will redirect and recommission us in the appropriate time.

In one of the darkest seasons of my life, it was the revelation of God's character that gave me back my hope. The enemy had been seeking to tell me that I was a failure, and as a result, hopelessness filled my soul. I didn't even have the strength to try anymore. That was when the Holy Spirit gently revealed to me God's faithfulness. I realized that even when I was without faith, He remained faithful.[12] Faithful is He who called me, and He would bring it to pass.[13] When I realized it was more about His faithfulness than mine, a confidence and rest in the Lord started to fill my soul. In a self-imposed wilderness, it is vital that we allow ourselves to rest and be refreshed in God.

God in the Wilderness

A self-imposed wilderness is a season typically marked by exhaustion. We are tired of fighting. Helplessness, hopelessness, or self-abasement has weighed us down. In this type of wilderness, we tend to experience physical and emotional tiredness and sometimes even thoughts of despair. This wilderness usually occurs after an event or season of intense exertion, and in our weariness, we run from the call of the Lord in our lives.

The Lord is not the initiator of this type of wilderness — we are, but it is not for good reasons. The important thing to know is that even here, God will come to our aid. He will show Himself to be compassionate and merciful with us. He will comfort and strengthen us and give us direction at the appropriate time. As the Lord works with us, we can participate with Him by receiving His rest and refreshment and allowing His character and nature to be established in our hearts.

Notes / Reference Scriptures

1. Revelation 2:20
2. Acts 7:23-25
3. Acts 7:27-28
4. Jonah 1:2-3
5. Jonah 1:17
6. Matthew 5:3-4
7. 1 Kings 19:14
8. John 18:18
9. 1 Kings 19:5-6
10. Mark 6:27-31
11. 1 Kings 19:5-7
12. 2 Timothy 2:13
13. 1 Thessalonians 5:24

9 God in the Wilderness: In Conclusion

Recently, I was talking with a young man who told me that his life had become nothing but a series of adversities. He couldn't understand why things had gotten so hard for him. As we talked about what he was going through, he shared a number of prophetic words that had been spoken over him, all of which had to do with his becoming a warrior in the spiritual realm.

I started laughing—gently, of course, so as not to upset him. Why was he surprised at the difficult events in his life? He was being trained as a warrior! He was in a wilderness of transition. "If you are going to be a warrior in the spirit," I told him, "you have to learn to fight to believe." He could rejoice in these opportunities to become the very thing God had spoken over him. He couldn't fulfill his destiny of being a warrior if he didn't have anything to fight. He couldn't be called an overcomer unless he actually overcame something.

All of us are destined to be conformed into the image of our Lord and Savior (Romans 8:29). We have the opportunity to allow the very nature of God to permeate our souls. As we journey through this world, we will encounter different types of adversities, most of which were designed by our adversary to hinder and distract us from our destinies. One of the adversities all of us will experience is the wilderness. It is not a question of if; it is a question of when and what kind. Whether the wilderness lasts several hours, several weeks, or a year—our response in the wilderness will help determine the direction of our lives.

There is no reason for us to fear, worry, or even be concerned when we realize we are in a wilderness. As we seek Him, God will work out to our benefit everything that happens in our lives, including these adversities. The important thing to learn is how to partner with Him, allowing the good He wants to bring to come about.

As you move forward, I want to encourage you. Our God is the God of all comfort. I used to think that comfort meant to ease or sedate the pain, but one day as I was about to undergo surgery, I realized that comfort actually means "one called alongside." God is the One who is always alongside us. He loves us and paid a huge price — He gave everything — to enable us to receive the best of His Kingdom. He purposed the best for us. He planned the best to occur. He redeems our mistakes so they cannot hold us back. He empowers and graces us to live out His good purposes and plans. He gives His Spirit to walk with us. He intercedes for us. He cheers us on.

And He waits for us at the finish line, so we can eternally enjoy Him as He enjoys us.

Anytime you face adversity, know that you can overcome it and extract out of it treasures that will last forever.

For additional information please visit our website:

www.dealingjesus.org

www.ingramcontent.com/pod-product-compliance
Lightning Source LLC
Chambersburg PA
CBHW020902090426
42736CB00008B/468